Going west from the forest at Hitteril Hill

OFFICIAL GUIDE

The Southern Upland Way

KEN ANDREW

WESTERN SECTION

COUNTRYSIDE COMMISSION FOR SCOTLAND
HMSO

First published 1984

Inside front cover
Dalveen Pass from Comb Head

Inside back cover
Glen Trool (Scottish Tourist Board)

Frontispiece
Sanquhar Post Office

Designed by HMSO Graphic Design/Edinburgh

Photographs by Ken Andrew

Cover and map illustrations by Bill Forbes

Front cover
Portpatrick Harbour
Back cover
Wanlockhead Beam Engine
Map cover
Cairnsmore of Carsphairn

ISBN 0 11 492362 0

Contents

SANQUHAR
POST OFFICE
SANQUHAR POST OFFICE
OLDEST IN GREAT BRITAIN
1763
YOUR
ELEPHONE ACCOUNT
MAY BE PAID AT
THIS OFFICE

Foreword

Foreword by Michael Ancram, MP, Minister for Home Affairs and the Environment at the Scottish Office.

The Southern Uplands, from Galloway to the Borders, represent for many people the 'undiscovered' face of Scotland. Yet this is an area rich in fine scenery, steeped in Scottish history and immortalised in our literature. I have been fortunate to have known many of these hills, lochs and valleys all my life and I believe that the opening of the Southern Upland Way long-distance footpath, running for 212 miles from Portpatrick on the south-west coast to Cockburnspath on the eastern seaboard, will bring great pleasure to many walkers, including our visitors from other countries.

This is the first east-west coast-to-coast long-distance footpath to have been officially designated in Britain and I have no doubt that it will stand comparison with Scotland's first long-distance route, the West Highland Way. The Southern Upland Way is, however, of quite distinct character, as well as being more than twice the length of the West Highland Way. The negotiation and development of this fine route has been completed in the remarkably short period of only five years, thanks to the enthusiasm of the planning authorities and the helpful attitude of the many landowners and tenants, farmers and foresters, who were involved.

This guide is a handsome and very readable companion for the walker and its maps are an essential aid for route-finding along the Way. I am therefore very pleased to introduce this publication, which will contribute a great deal to increased enjoyment – and increased understanding – of the Southern Uplands of Scotland.

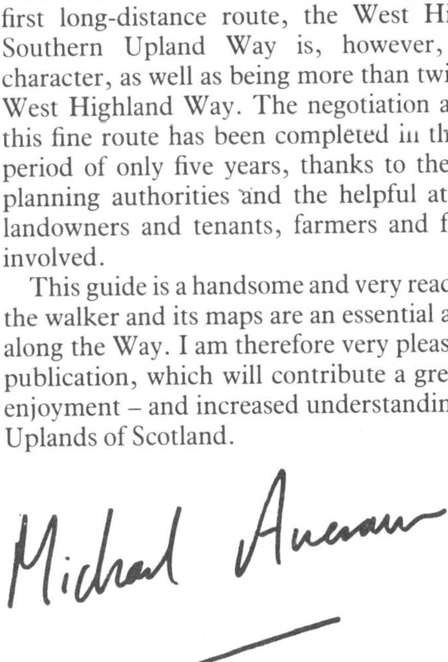

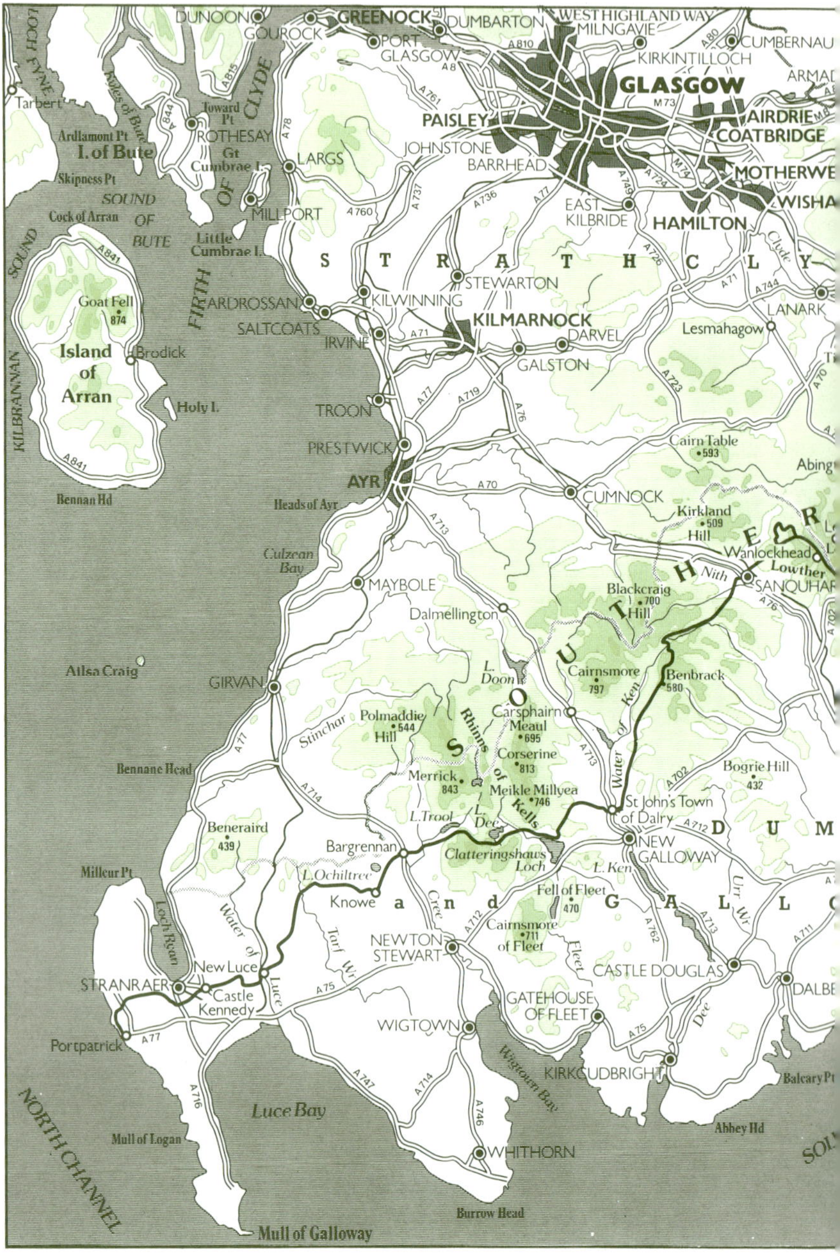

LOCH FYNE
Tarbert
DUNOON
GOUROCK
GREENOCK
PORT GLASGOW
DUMBARTON
WEST HIGHLAND WAY
MILNGAVIE
KIRKINTILLOCH
CUMBERNAU
GLASGOW
PAISLEY
JOHNSTONE
BARRHEAD
AIRDRIE
COATBRIDGE
MOTHERWE
WISHA
HAMILTON
EAST KILBRIDE
Kyles of Bute
Toward Pt
ROTHESAY
Ardlamont Pt
I. of Bute
Skipness Pt
SOUND OF BUTE
Cock of Arran
Gt Cumbrae I.
MILLPORT
Little Cumbrae I.
FIRTH OF CLYDE
LARGS
KILBRANNAN SOUND
Goat Fell 874
Island of Arran
Brodick
Holy I.
ARDROSSAN
SALTCOATS
IRVINE
KILWINNING
STEWARTON
KILMARNOCK
DARVEL
GALSTON
STRATHCLYDE
LANARK
Lesmahagow
TROON
PRESTWICK
AYR
Bennan Hd
Heads of Ayr
Culzean Bay
CUMNOCK
Cairn Table 593
Kirkland Hill 509
Wanlockhead
Lowther
Nith
SANQUHAR
MAYBOLE
Dalmellington
Blackcraig Hill 700
Ailsa Craig
GIRVAN
L. Doon
Cairnsmore 797
Benbrack 580
Polmaddie Hill 544
Rhinns of Kells
Carsphairn
Meaul 695
Corserine 813
Stinchar
Bennane Head
Merrick 843
Meikle Millyea 746
Water of Ken
Bogrie Hill 432
St John's Town of Dalry
L. Trool
L. Dee
Beneraird 439
Bargrennan
Clatteringshaws Loch
NEW GALLOWAY
L. Ken
SOUTHERN UPLAND WAY
DUMFRIES and GALLOWAY
Milleur Pt
L. Ochiltree
Knowe
Fell of Fleet 470
Loch Ryan
Water of Luce
Tarf Wr
Cree
Cairnsmore of Fleet 711
NEWTON STEWART
Urr Wr
CASTLE DOUGLAS
DALBE
STRANRAER
New Luce
Castle Kennedy
GATEHOUSE OF FLEET
Portpatrick
WIGTOWN
Wigtown Bay
KIRKCUDBRIGHT
Dee
Balcary Pt
Luce Bay
Abbey Hd
NORTH CHANNEL
Mull of Logan
WHITHORN
Burrow Head
Mull of Galloway
SOL

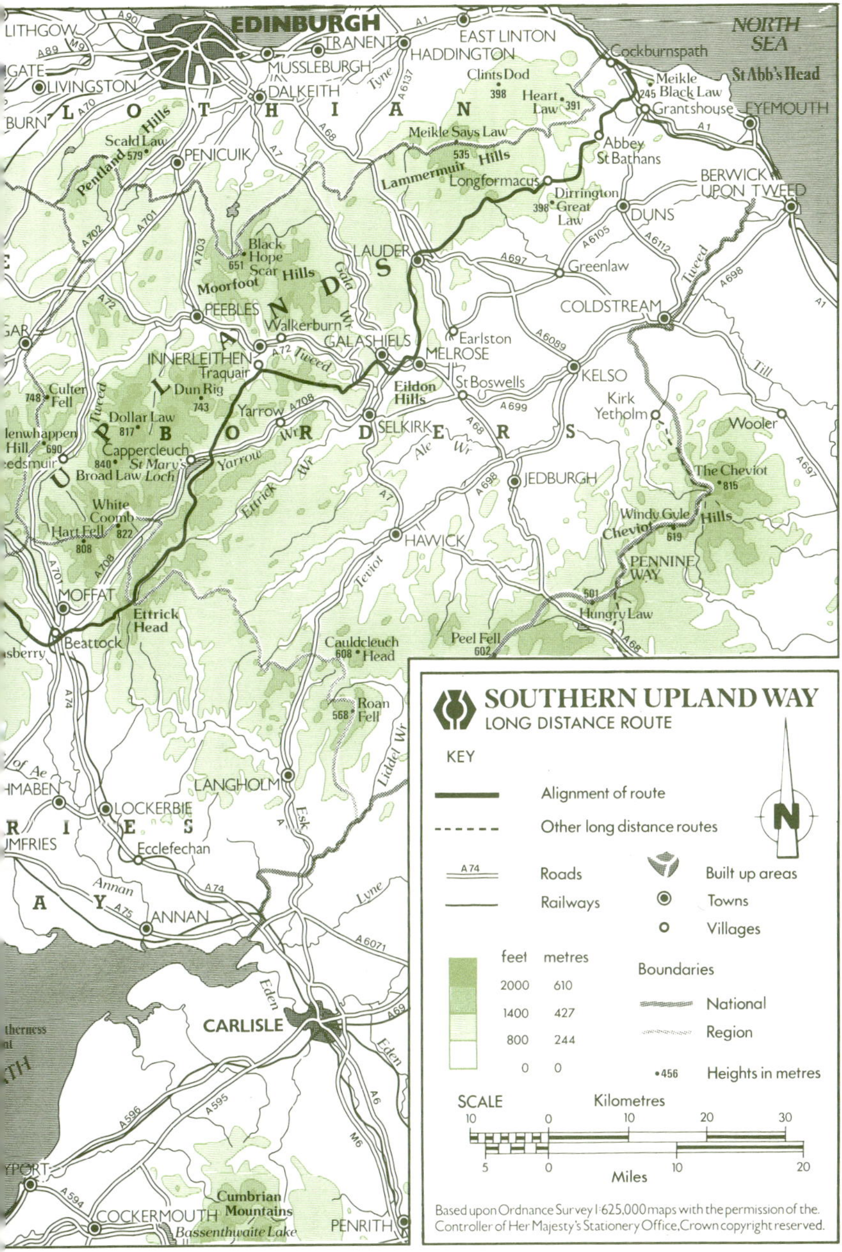
EDINBURGH
NORTH SEA
St Abb's Head
EYEMOUTH
LITHGOW
LIVINGSTON
TRANENT
MUSSLEBURGH
DALKEITH
HADDINGTON
EAST LINTON
Cockburnspath
Meikle
245 Black Law
Grantshouse
Clints Dod
398
Heart Law 391
L O T H I A N
Scald Law
579
Pentland Hills
PENICUIK
Meikle Says Law
535
Lammermuir Hills
Longformacus
Abbey St Bathans
BERWICK UPON TWEED
Dirrington
398 Great Law
DUNS
Black Hope Scar
651
Moorfoot Hills
LAUDER
Greenlaw
COLDSTREAM
PEEBLES
Walkerburn
GALASHIELS
Earlston
INNERLEITHEN
Traquair
MELROSE
KELSO
Culter Fell
748
Dun Rig
743
Eildon Hills
St Boswells
Kirk Yetholm
Dollar Law
817
Yarrow
SELKIRK
Wooler
Hill 690
Cappercleuch
840
St Mary's Loch
Broad Law
JEDBURGH
The Cheviot
815
White Coomb
Hart Fell 822
808
Windy Gyle
619
Cheviot Hills
HAWICK
PENNINE WAY
MOFFAT
501
Hungry Law
Ettrick Head
Beattock
Cauldcleuch Head
608
Peel Fell
602
Roan Fell
568
U P L A N D S
B O R D E R S
LANGHOLM
LOCKERBIE
Ecclefechan
D U M F R I E S
ANNAN
CARLISLE
COCKERMOUTH
Cumbrian Mountains
Bassenthwaite Lake
PENRITH
Tweed
Gala Wr
Yarrow Wr
Ettrick Wr
Ale Wr
Teviot
Till
Esk
Liddel Wr
Annan
Lyne
Eden
A1
A7
A68
A72
A74
A75
A697
A698
A699
A708
A6071
A595
A596
A594
M6
SOUTHERN UPLAND WAY
LONG DISTANCE ROUTE
KEY
Alignment of route
Other long distance routes
Roads
Railways
Built up areas
Towns
Villages
feet metres
2000 610
1400 427
800 244
0 0
Boundaries
National
Region
•456 Heights in metres
SCALE
Kilometres
10 0 10 20 30
5 0 10 20
Miles
N
Based upon Ordnance Survey 1:625,000 maps with the permission of the Controller of Her Majesty's Stationery Office, Crown copyright reserved.

Portpatrick Harbour

Introduction

The Southern Upland Way is Britain's first official east-west coast-to-coast long-distance footpath. It is the third Scottish long-distance route to be promoted by the Countryside Commission for Scotland and the first in southern Scotland – although a short stretch of the Pennine Way extends into south Scotland, with its terminus at Kirk Yetholm in the Borders.

Under the Countryside (Scotland) Act 1967, the Countryside Commission for Scotland is given responsibility for preparing and submitting reports to the Secretary of State for Scotland on the development of long-distance routes where it considers that the public should be enabled to make extensive cross-country journeys on foot, avoiding public roads wherever possible. The very popular 152km (95 miles) West Highland Way between Milngavie and Fort William, opened in 1980, and the 96km (60 miles) Speyside Way between Spey Bay on the Moray Firth and Glenmore near Aviemore (the latter as yet only open along part of its length) are both in the Highlands of Scotland.

On 13 July 1979, the Secretary of State for Scotland gave his approval to the Commission's proposals for the Southern Upland Way, running some 340km (212 miles) from Portpatrick on the south-west coast of Scotland – to Cockburnspath on the eastern seaboard. The Southern Upland Way passes through three of Scotland's local authority regions – Dumfries and Galloway, Strathclyde, and Borders. The work of implementing the route, the access negotiations with the many proprietors, and the provision of bridges, stiles, waymarkers and information boards, has been undertaken by these Regional Councils in a remarkably short period of time. It says much for their energy and enthusiasm – and the work of Royal Engineer units of the Army, Scottish Conservation Projects volunteers and local contractors, together with Manpower Services Commission funded

Community Enterprise Project teams – that the route is now available for the use and enjoyment of walkers. Much of the route of the Southern Upland Way follows existing paths and tracks – some of them of ancient origin. Particular thought has been given to the safety of walkers, the interests of wildlife and conservation, and the existing land-uses of farming, forestry and sport. The Way incorporates coastal cliff-top paths, old drove roads and coffin roads, former military roads, forest and farm roads, river and lochside paths, disused railway routes, hill ridges, moorland trails, industrial trails, Roman roads, ecclesiastical roads, coaching roads and – where no route previously existed – it has made its own. The route passes over high hilltops, through deep valleys and across wide moors; it enters towns and villages, crosses trunk roads and railway lines, traverses forests, grouse moors, arable farms and sheep and cattle country. Some stretches of the Way – such as the south side of Glen Trool and the Minchmuir – have been popular leisure-walking routes for generations, whilst the Border Walkway, from Galashiels to Moffat, is a modern concept which has been adopted to the benefit of all. The Southern Upland Way has thus unified a great variety of routes, both ancient and modern, into a noble and mighty idea, providing for walkers a healthy, enjoyable and challenging experience.

As with other long-distance footpaths, the Southern Upland Way will have its critics who will seize on imperfections in the route, and in this Guide. Those critics may suggest that many long-distance walkers are potential vandals, litter-louts and a menace to themselves and to others. Walkers will therefore have the responsibility of proving the critics wrong by using commonsense, courtesy and consideration during their trek across Scotland. No-one would claim that a new footpath over 200 miles in length can be established and used without some adverse effects. What can safely be asserted is that the Southern Upland Way offers a great new opportunity to many walkers. It will introduce many people to exciting new places, and will also help to provide a small, but welcome, boost to the tourist economy of southern Scotland.

There is, strictly speaking, no such thing on the British mainland as a truly natural wilderness. Man's influence is evident in every landscape – even in the renowned Highlands. As in the Highlands, armies have marched and counter-marched over the Southern Uplands, and countless numbers of sheep and cattle have been herded across these hills and through the valleys to the southern markets. Over the centuries these human activities, along with agricultural, sporting and forestry developments, have had a profound effect on the countryside – but the hills are still standing, the lochs are still there and the rivers still flow. Given proper use and wise management, the land will also survive the feet of today's leisure-walkers. In looking at recreational developments of this kind, we have to consider all the influences at work: geology, climate, population changes, social customs, political history, varying patterns of land-use – and the effects of industry. The story of a country's landscape is a complex fabric, woven from many strands. The life and history of Scotland in its many facets, tragic and heroic, is written along the length of the Southern Upland Way, demonstrating a cultural heritage of incredibly rich dimensions. Those who walk this route in its entirety will enjoy a unique educational experience – as well as becoming members of an elite group who can reflect on the sense of physical achievement – and spiritual uplift – which comes from having crossed Scotland from coast to coast on their own two feet.

Walking the Way

A 340km (212 miles) walk is not easy – and it must be stressed at the outset that the Southern Upland Way traverses some particularly hard and gruelling stretches of countryside. The West Highland Way and the Speyside Way, in common with many other classic walking routes in Scotland, tend to follow the valleys and lines of least resistance in the landscape. By contrast, the Southern Upland Way, in addition to being more than twice the length of the West Highland Way, has to work its passage *across* the valleys. A study of a map of Scotland will make this clear. The north to south tendency of rivers, roads and railways is more pronounced in the Southern Uplands than elsewhere. Whilst many miles of the Southern Upland Way are on the level, on tarred roads or good footpaths and tracks, many miles are also up and downhill, often through rough vegetation and over generally soft ground. Let no-one be under the misapprehension that, because this walk is set outside the Highlands of Scotland, it can be treated lightly. Those who intend to walk the entire route in one expedition must be very fit and have considerable hillwalking experience. Those who lack this fitness and experience should tackle the route in easier stages. Since the Southern Upland Way crosses the grain of the country, it frequently leaves the valleys and lines of communication behind, threading its way through areas where population is sparse and transport and shelter practically non-existent. For these reasons, walkers who come to the Way ill-equipped cannot simply opt out when the going gets tough. Make no mistake about it, this is a big route in more ways than one.

Direction

This guide, published in two volumes, describes the Way from west to east – and walkers are strongly advised to tackle the route in this direction if they possibly can – starting at Portpatrick and finishing at Cockburnspath. Walking north-eastwards, the sun is generally at your back and the colour and details of the landscape are more easily seen to the front. The prevailing winds are south-westerly so it is as well to have the weather behind you, too. Walkers tackling the route from east to west will find the accompanying route map provides the best way of navigating the Way in the reverse direction to the guide description.

Weather

Southern Upland weather comes mainly from the Atlantic Ocean. The prevailing westerly winds which affect Scotland are generally very moist after journeying across thousands of miles of sea. Cloudy conditions, grey skies and rain are common – but beautiful spells of sunshine, giving sparkling landscapes, can occur between the fronts and are not so rare as many people may imagine. However, settled conditions rarely last for long, so good judgement is required in choosing the ideal time to tackle the Southern Upland Way! The walker is likely to experience an interesting mix of wind, rain and sunshine on a complete traverse of the Way – although extended periods of settled weather could turn up, giving either a heatwave, unremitting gloom and rain or – ideally – cool, clear and fresh conditions. Rainfall varies across the country, according to height and distance from the coast. From an annual average of about 1000mm (40 inches) at Portpatrick, the average rainfall rises to about 2000mm at Glen Trool and tails off gradually beyond the Lowthers to under 1000mm in the Lammermuirs, down to about 750mm at Cockburnspath. On the lee side of the hills, the east tends to get much less cloud and more sun than the west, but when the wind is from an easterly quarter, the position is reversed. The increasing risk of rain and cloud which comes with altitude should always be borne in mind. It can be a fine day in the valleys or on the coasts, whilst on the hills it is wet and cloudy. The east coast tends to suffer from haar – sea mist – at times and these conditions can prevail on days when it is warm and sunny inland.

February to June can be very dry months, when great care needs to be taken against causing fires, especially in the vicinity of forests and grasslands. July and August may be disappointingly cloudy or hazy, whilst the November to January period tends to be wet and – of course – dark. The risk of being caught out in the dark is something the winter walker needs to guard against. The light can be fading by very early afternoon on a misty hill in mid-winter and, given the substantial distances involved in walking the Southern Upland Way, careful planning is required. No hard and fast rules can be laid down and no guarantees can be given for Southern Upland weather. Generally, however, late spring and early summer are the best periods, with long hours of daylight, reasonable temperatures, fresh growth to brighten the countryside, few midges about, the bracken yet to uncoil above head-height, the shepherd's anxieties over his lambs have lessened, and the vegetation and paths are drying out and allowing faster walking progress.

Novice walkers are safer to confine their outings to the summer months, taking the risk that it could still be cloudy or unpleasantly hot and muggy with attendant hordes of tormenting insects – for which a repellent is necessary. Heat-stroke is another risk and headgear of some kind should be carried in summer. Bare flesh should not be toasted in the sun for too long unless it is used to it, and extra clothes should be carried to replace shorts – and cover up white legs which are beginning to feel the heat. Each season has its own pleasures and miseries and the fit and experienced walker who is not afraid of bouts of rough weather and some discomfort can enjoy the more transient but colourful days, the short-lived autumn colours, the winter frosts and snows, the rainbows and cloudscapes.

The walker by now will have gathered that the weather is the crucial factor on the Southern Upland Way! Enjoyment and success go with good weather so try to get your weather right by studying the forecasts. Satellite pictures on TV are useful in showing the approach of broken skies and clear weather to the British Isles, and TV weather maps can give an idea of what to expect. The most useful radio forecasts are probably those at the start and end of the day on BBC Radio 4 at 12.10am, 6am, 6.55am and 7.55am – or at 6.55am on Radio 3. The shipping forecasts at 12.15am and 6.25am on Radio 4 are also very useful, giving reports of existing weather at various stations around Britain, with the Southern Uplands likely to catch similar conditions downwind within a day. Particular attention should be paid to the shipping forecasts for the areas Irish Sea and Malin – which lie off Galloway, and Forth and Tyne.

Up-to-the-minute forecasts can be obtained by telephoning Meteorological Offices at Edinburgh Airport, the Glasgow Weather Centre, Prestwick, Newcastle or Pitreavie. The numbers will be found at the start of the telephone directory. This is an excellent service which can provide a forecast tailor-made for any walker.

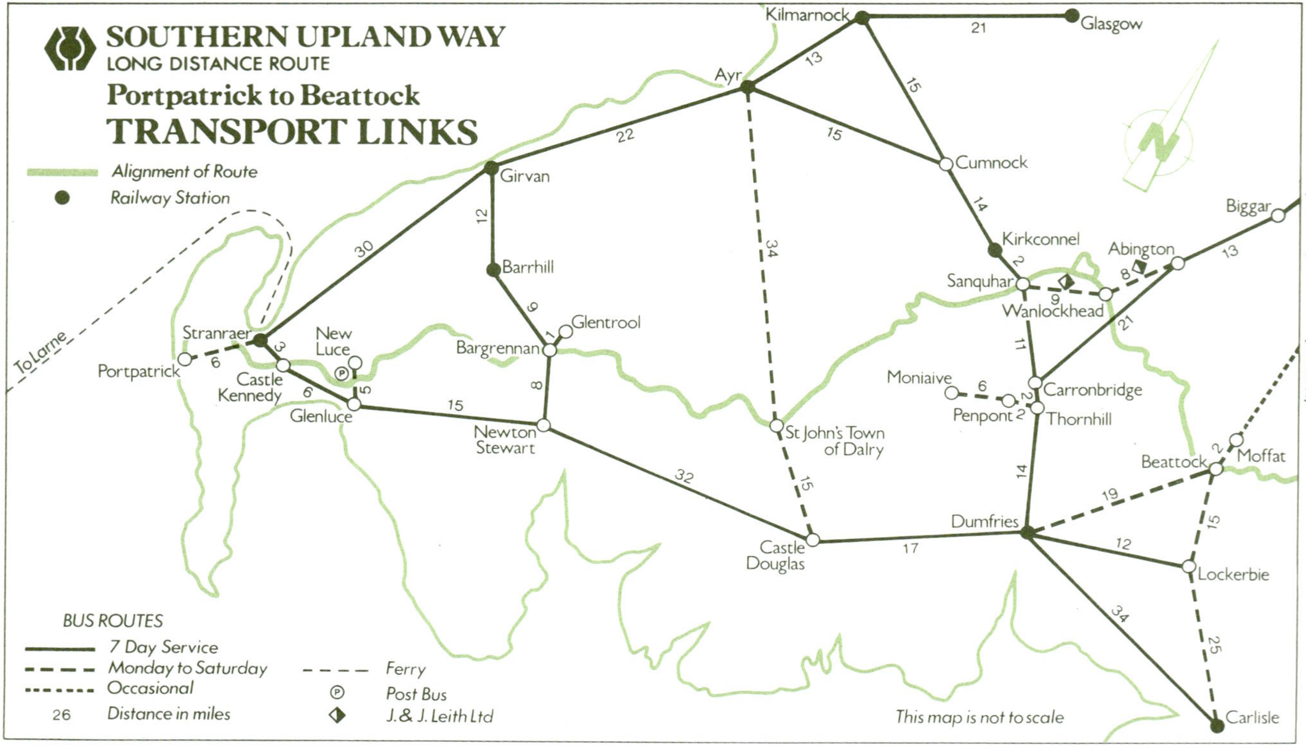

NB: Bus and rail services are subject to change. Walkers should check the up-to-date situation before setting out.

Following the Way

This guide has been written in two parts, Volume I covering the western section of the route, and Volume II, the east. Each volume has its accompanying route map of four sections. Map section four of Vol. I overlaps with map section one of Vol. II. Walkers planning to undertake the whole length – or large sections of the Way – therefore need both Volumes. Vol. I (West) covers the Way from Portpatrick to Beattock and Vol. II (East) leads on from Beattock to Cockburnspath.

In addition to the two sets of maps and the two volumes of the official guide, walkers also have the assistance of signposts and waymarkers. The dark brown posts carry a thistle within a hexagon symbol, which is the standard identification for a designated long-distance footpath in Scotland. These have been placed at strategic points along the Way to indicate changes of direction, and to confirm that the walker is on the correct line where the route is not obvious. The waymarkers have been erected by the regional planning authorities, who have tried to keep them to a minimum consistent with safety.

Yellow arrows are painted on the waymark posts to show direction whilst the taller signposts are situated at junctions or where the route leaves a road and extra guidance is needed. Remember, waymarkers are a fair-weather aid. The ability to navigate with map and compass is essential: in bad visibility you won't see the markers! Walkers not able to navigate accurately in mist should not attempt the long stretches of hill country on the Way. Stiles and wooden bridges of a standard pattern can also be recognised as route-markers in some places – and where markers are absent, walkers can expect to follow the obvious route, be it a stone wall, fence, forest road or path, until the next waymarker post is seen.

The route maps designed for the Southern Upland Way are crucial for navigation. These have been specially prepared by the Ordnance Survey from its 1:50,000 series. Because of the south-west to north-east alignment of the Way, seven standard OS maps would normally have had to be purchased to provide coverage for this route. To keep bulk and weight to a minimum, the four route map sections accompanying each of the two volumes of the guide show the Way within a relatively narrow corridor. The difficulty of mapping this trans-Scotland footpath has necessitated the maps being skewed at 30°. This puts the north to south grid lines at an angle to the edges of the map sheets – but compass bearings are still taken in relation to the grid lines, despite their unorthodox appearance. It is worth repeating that walkers should have a good knowledge of how to use the map and compass before tackling the entire route – or the remoter stretches of it.

Times and Distances

It is not possible to give a useful estimate of how long a complete traverse of the Southern Upland Way will take. Individual walkers travel at their own speed – and performance will vary considerably, depending upon weather and underfoot conditions. In cool, dry conditions, walkers will romp along much faster than in hot, humid weather – or when the ground is wet. Walking in in shirts and shorts will generally be quicker than in rainwear. Navigation in mist can be a slow business, whilst advancing into a headwind is rather more difficult than being bowled along by a tailwind! Rain, wind, sleet or snow – as well as causing discomfort – will hinder access to rucksacks and pockets and make it difficult to use maps and guides. A few walkers may see the Way as some kind of race to be run against the clock or the calendar. It would be wiser not to do so. The normal walker can expect to spend somewhere between 10 and 20 days on the route, depending on fitness.

The guide divides the Way into 15 distinct stretches – seven in the western half (Volume I) and eight in the east (Volume II). These stretches are, however, of unequal length and difficulty. A number of the sections can be done easily by a family party inside a day – but several are very long – the longest being 43km (27 miles) – and very demanding. Sensible walkers will allow two days for these lengthy stretches.

Naismith's Rule can be used to work out a very rough estimate for time and distance. This suggests allowing one hour for every 5km (3 miles) to be walked, plus half-an-hour for every 300m (1000 feet) to be climbed. Circumstances and weather can play havoc with this estimate, of course, and walkers are cautioned to allow themselves plenty of extra time.

Accommodation and Facilities along the Way

A good night's rest is a vital element in achieving a successful day's walking. Most Southern Upland Way walkers will need to find between 10 and 20 different overnight resting places between the west and east coasts. Inevitably, there is a good choice in some localities – and a dearth of facilities in others. The situation will always be subject to alteration and the pages of this guide can therefore give only a general indication of the location and type of accommodation available, together with outline details of other services and facilities important

Accommodation and Facilities along the Way: Portpatrick—Beattock

	information	accommodation	camp site	youth hostel	bothy	snacks/meals	toilets	shops	telephone
Portpatrick		●	●			●	●	●	●
Stranraer	●	●	●			●	●	●	●
Castle Kennedy		●				●	●	●	●
(Glenluce)		●	●				●	●	●
New Luce		●				●		●	●
Bargrennan		●	●			●			●
(Glentrool village)								●	●
Glen Trool			●				●	●	
(Newton Stewart)	●	●		●		●	●	●	●
Loch Dee					●				
Dalry		●				●	●	●	●
(New Galloway)		●				●		●	●
(Kendoon)				●					
(Carsphairn)		●				●		●	●
Sanquhar		●	●			●	●	●	●
Wanlockhead				●			●	●	●
(Leadhills)		●				●		●	●
Beattock		●	●			●		●	●
(Moffat)	●	●	●			●	●	●	●

Settlements shown in brackets are off the route.

to walkers. A Southern Upland Way accommodation list is issued free by the Countryside Commission for Scotland, from which the up-to-date position can more readily be checked. Copies are available from the Commission on request (address on inside back page) or at local tourist information centres. Additional guidance on holiday accommodation can be obtained from the Scottish Tourist Board, 23 Ravelston Terrace, Edinburgh EH4 3EU or at local tourist information centres. The Board publishes a range of useful accommodation guides. Many places close down in the winter months and many will be fully booked in the high summer. Walkers will save themselves a lot of trouble – and extra walking – if they seek and plan their accommodation in advance through tourist information centres. Registers will be kept of some of the beds available in the locality – and in many cases staff may be able to make a telephone booking, saving walkers the torment of walking around town and country looking at 'No Vacancies' signs. For current information, contact: Dumfries and Galloway Tourist Board, Douglas House, Newton Stewart (Tel: 0671 2549) and Scottish Borders Tourist Board, Municipal Buildings, High Street, Selkirk (Tel: 0750 20555).

Youth Hostels

There are six youth hostels which could be of use to Southern Upland Way walkers. They are provided by the Scottish Youth Hostels Association and are available only to members of that Association. However, walkers can join the SYHA at any of the hostels by paying a modest enrolment fee. Overnight charges are also very modest, varying according to the member's age and the grade of the hostel. The hostels on or near the Way are:

Portpatrick—Beattock

Minnigaff (Newton Stewart) (GR 411663): Grade 3, 44 beds, 25 March-1 October.

Kendoon (GR 616883): Grade 3, 38 beds, 15 May-1 October, also Friday, Saturday and Sunday at Easter, and Saturdays from Easter to 15 May.

Wanlockhead (GR 874131): Grade 3, 30 beds, 25 March-1 October and Saturdays in winter.

Beattock—Cockburnspath

Broadmeadows (GR 417303): Grade 3, 28 beds, 25 March-1 October.

Melrose (GR 550340): Grade 2, 90 beds, 9 March-30 October. Friday and Saturday in winter and normally at New Year. Closed during November.

Coldingham (GR 915664): Grade 2, 68 beds, 25 March-1 October.

Hostels are generally busiest at the weekends and in the summer months and during Easter holidays. Bookings can be made in advance to ensure admittance. For details of membership and a current handbook, write to: Secretary, SYHA, 7 Glebe Crescent, Stirling FK8 2JA.

Bothies

The White Laggan (GR 466775) at Loch Dee – and Over Phawhope (GR 182082) north-east of Ettrick Head – are simple, unlocked bothies providing wind and watertight shelter, but lacking in facilities. These bothies are available for use by walkers but they could be crowded at times.

Camping

Many Way-walkers will be campers and backpackers and a waterproof tent with fly-sheet and sewn-in groundsheet is strongly recommended. Campers should use recognised camp sites where these are available along the Way. Campers should always seek permission before pitching their tents and random camping is specifically prohibited in some areas, for example in the Galloway Forest Park, except at the Forestry Commission's Caldons Camp Site. Avoid camping anywhere near plantations; where stock are grazing, or in the vicinity of grouse moors. Attitudes to campers – who could represent a large proportion of all Way walkers – will be determined by the behaviour of the campers themselves and courtesy, tidiness and consideration for others are more likely to lead to a welcome than are thoughtless behaviour and leaving litter behind. Campers will have a special responsibility in ensuring a welcome for those walkers who come after them.

Transport

Public transport in the Southern Uplands normally involves buses. The Way crosses or passes close to a number of bus routes, which will allow walkers to join or leave the Way. The south of Scotland is thinly populated and buses are infrequent – and may be non-existent in some areas. A map showing the main transport links will be found on page 18. The Portpatrick-Beattock section of the Way is served by Western Scottish bus services and the Beattock-Cockburnspath section by Eastern Scottish. Additional services are provided by local operators such as J. & J. Leith Ltd, Sanquhar, and Creightons of Moffat. Post buses carrying mail – and a very limited number of passengers – operate at New Luce, Longformacus and Abbey St Bathans. Railways remaining in the Southern Uplands either tend to skirt round the periphery of the Way – or hurtle non-stop across it. Few railway stations exist anywhere near the Way. Bus and rail timetables are subject to regular revision so it is advisable to check in advance. Details of main bus services can be obtained from the Travel Centre, Buchanan Bus Station, Killermont Street, Glasgow G2 3NP. Timetables for other services may be obtained at tourist information centres.

Clothing and Equipment

Allowing for a fortnight's walking – much of it in the hills – requires a good deal of thought to be given to the safe minimum amount of equipment required. The more weight you carry, the slower is your progress – and the longer you take for the journey. Thus you need extra clothing and equipment! It is a vicious circle. Work out what is the minimum amount of gear you need, allowing for season and probable weather, and then add a margin for error and unforeseen setbacks. Good quality hill-walking kit is essential for those tackling any substantial part of the route, or even one section in cold, wet or changeable weather conditions. You *might* survive in shorts and sandshoes over some parts of the route in summer, if you are lucky with the weather, but it would be foolish to attempt to do so without having reserves of warm and waterproof clothing in your rucksack. Several lighter layers of clothing are better than one thick one, so that you can add or take off to regulate your temperature. Wool is much warmer than synthetic fibres.

The terrain of the Way makes its own local climate and, as the environment changes, it will be necessary to alter your clothing accordingly. If you wear shorts, carry warm trousers or breeches (not jeans) in reserve, to cover up against cold, rain, wind and sunburn, as well as nettles and midges. A windproof and waterproof anorak can be combined with a lightweight cagoule and over-trousers to protect you against the worst weather. Carry a woollen cap or balaclava, and take gloves, unless you are in a heatwave – when you will still need headgear for protection against the sun. Remember the spare sweater. Good hill-walking boots with moulded rubber soles are the most suitable form of footwear, along with several pairs of woollen socks – and spare dry pairs. Plastic and leather soles slip on grass slopes and wet rock and are dangerous. Anklets or gaiters are useful for keeping out mud, water and snow. Do not forget a spare pair of laces.

The route map, compass, whistle and a small first-aid kit are essential and walkers should know how to use them. A simple blister left untreated can cause misery. Midge repellent can help to stop you being tortured between June and October, and a torch and spare batteries should be carried. A bivouac bag or large plastic sack could save your life in an emergency. Campers will have the heaviest burden as – apart from the tent – they will need a good quality sleeping bag, plus stove, fuel and cooking equipment.

A comfortable, well-packed rucksack is essential for all walkers – but try to avoid too heavy a load. Finally, if you plan to walk between December and April, an ice-axe could be a valuable friend.

Services and Supplies

Adequate supplies of food are essential to maintain energy. Your stores can be topped-up along the Way where shops are available, but they can be few and far between and hold limited stocks. Planning your supplies in advance is important. Day walkers can exist on energy foods such as jam sandwiches, chocolate and glucose, with a flask of soup, coffee or tea as a non-essential extra. The long-distance walker will need a greater variety of lightweight packaged foods. Water should not be drunk from burns or lochs below dwellings or in the neighbourhood of sheep and cattle pens, but in other circumstances the water is generally pure and safe. The services we take for granted in the city – banks, post offices, doctors and police – are less numerous along the Way and walkers should allow for this in their route planning.

Safety on the Hills

Follow the Mountain Code:

Think carefully before you go alone
Leave written word of your route with someone responsible and report your progress at the first opportunity
Plan within your capabilities
Know the local weather forecast
Watch the weather and adjust your plans wisely
Be properly equipped
Know how to use map and compass
Know the mountain distress signal – six regular whistles/flashes a minute, repeated at one-minute intervals
Know simple first-aid and the symptoms of exposure
Eat a little from time to time to maintain energy
Keep alert all day

In the event of accidents or emergencies, find the nearest telephone and dial 999, asking for POLICE.

The Country Code

Many people will walk the Southern Upland Way. The quality of their experience – and the welcome they receive – will depend upon the behaviour of those who go before them. Each has a responsibility to observe the Country Code, which is the key to ensuring happy relationships between walkers and those who live and work along the route.

Guard Against all Risk of Fire
The Southern Upland Way passes through substantial areas of woodland. Fires can start in forests and woodlands, and on grasslands and heather, at any season of the year – even in winter. Fire is an indiscriminate and unpredictable hazard, endangering people, wildlife and scenery. It can destroy in a few hours, at great cost, that which has taken decades to grow. Camp fires should not be lit at all along the Way. The greatest care should be taken with stoves, keeping them well away from combustible material – and never, ever, left unattended.

Fasten all Gates
Where gates are used, fasten them securely behind you to prevent animals straying.

Keep your Dogs under Close Control
You are urged to leave dogs at home and not take them on the Southern Upland Way at all. The Way passes through lambing and stock-grazing areas at almost every stage of the journey and even docile dogs on a lead can upset stock very easily and cause great harm. Walkers will have enough problems on the Way without having to worry about the dog.

Keep to Public Paths across Farmland
The route of the Way has been agreed. There is no need to drift from the path into crops and pastures. Remember, grass is also a valuable crop to the farmer.

Use Gates and Stiles to cross Fences, Hedges and Walls
If walkers use the stiles provided it will not be necessary to clamber over fences and dykes, except where special crossing points have been built into the structure.

Leave Livestock, Crops and Machinery Alone
Machinery in the countryside can be dangerous. Try not to interfere with farming or forestry operations.

Take your Litter Home
Those on a single day's walk should take all their litter home. Walkers on longer outings should carry the minimum of tins and bottles, and dispose of them at service centres. Do not leave any litter in the countryside and try to avoid contributing to overflowing litter bins in rural areas.

Help to Keep all Water Clean

Numerous burns along the corridor of the Way supply individual houses or feed reservoirs for public water supply to communities within – and beyond – the Southern Uplands. Take care, particularly when camping, not to cause pollution. Do not allow your rubbish or unused food to find its way into burns, lochs or reservoirs.

Protect Wildlife, Plants and Trees

Bring back photographs, not specimens. Avoid disturbing birds and animals and do not trample plants or young trees.

Take Special Care on Country Roads

The Way uses a great number of country roads. Normally they are very quiet but for your own safety keep well to the right side of the road facing any potential traffic, and be especially careful at corners. Wear light-coloured clothing or carry a torch in poor light.

Make No Unnecessary Noise

Going quietly will allow you to see more wildlife – and will add to the enjoyment of others. Loud transistor radios will not endear the owner to fellow-walkers or local inhabitants!

Enjoy the Countryside and Respect its Life and Work

Much of the enjoyment of the Southern Upland Way will come from meeting those whose livelihood depends upon the land you walk on. There is much to learn – and much to see. The psychological separation between town and country is slowly shrinking: the Southern Upland Way walker who is considerate will make a valuable contribution to an increased understanding between urban and rural dwellers.

Lambing

Walkers are asked to take particular care during the lambing season which stretches from January on low ground farms, to May on the hill farms. If ewes or lambs are encountered during this period, avoid at all cost disturbing them. Pregnant ewes can easily lose their unborn lambs if surprised or distressed. Please *don't* pick up 'lost' lambs: they're not. Go round rather than through flocks of sheep at all times. Stand still if sheep show signs of nervousness. Do not under any circumstances take dogs anywhere near them.

Cattle are also likely to be encountered on the Way and the same care should be taken with them. They tend to be curious and may advance rather than retreat! Don't panic and run – unless an animal is obviously aggressive. Cows and bullocks will frequently run up, stop and take a good look at you. Avoid excitement or you will transfer that to the animal also. In the event of meeting a bull, ram or other animal you are not sure of, go round it if possible with an eye to escape routes, or retreat and seek another path.

Grouse Shooting

Where the Southern Upland Way crosses grouse moors, please keep to the footpath – and during the grouse shooting season, which starts on 12 August, avoid disturbance to a shoot and risk to yourself.

Countryside Ranger Services

Borders Regional Council and Dumfries and Galloway Regional Council operate countryside ranger services based on the Southern Upland Way. If you encounter any difficulties or have comments or suggestions, contact:

Countryside Ranger Service,
Borders Regional Council,
Department of Physical Planning,
Regional Headquarters,
Newtown St. Boswells,
Roxburghshire.

Countryside Ranger Service,
Dumfries and Galloway Regional Council,
Department of Physical Planning,
Council Buildings,
Dumfries.

The Rhins

PORTPATRICK—CASTLE KENNEDY

DISTANCE: 21½km (13½ miles) HEIGHT RANGE: 0–160m

This is an easy walk through farming territory for much of the distance, with stretches of terrain involving cliff-tops, shoreline, grass and heather grazings, and woodlands. The Way mainly follows paths, farm tracks and minor roads. This part of the route lends itself to the short family outing provided parties wear proper non-slip footwear, children are safeguarded at all times, and inexperienced parties are prepared to turn back at potential difficulties and before going too far from their base.

Care is required on the roads although traffic is generally very light. The cliff-top sections require special care, with stray golf-balls presenting an extra hazard, but the paths are broad, well maintained and fenced where there is a danger of straying to the shoreline at Killantringan Lighthouse.

This stretch of the route provides a well-balanced introduction to the Southern Upland Way, with splendid scenery right at the start. However, a bit of alertness is called for in route-finding, with frequent changes of direction and scenery, and a wide variety of underfoot conditions.

Escape routes back to base are frequently met, to aid walkers gauge their readiness in safety for the more serious work of the Southern Upland Way ahead. There is even a west coast to east coast element about this section, crossing the spine of the Rhins almost to the sea-inlet of Loch Ryan in a mini-rehearsal for a trans-Scotland expedition.

The Rhins is the name given to the peninsula of land at the south-west corner of Scotland, stretching from the Mull of Galloway to Milleur Point at the mouth of Loch Ryan. It is joined to the rest of Scotland by a low neck of land barely 20 metres above sea-level, which has been subjected through

Portpatrick and the Mull of Galloway from the north-west

time to great change, including inundation, uplift, scouring by the ice sheets, and land-building both by deposition of material by the glaciers and by wind-blown sand. If the Antarctic ice-cap melted, the Rhins could become an island off the coast of Scotland again. The proximity of the area to the warm current of the North Atlantic Drift gives it a very mild climate which is exploited in the Botanic Gardens at Port Logan on the west coast.

The crossing of the Rhins by the Southern Upland Way begins at Portpatrick, which has that much-painted, well-maintained look about it, typical of the trim fishing villages where the locals have learned to keep up their guard against the havoc wrought by storms. The village has a legendary connection with St Patrick, the patron saint of Ireland, but in 1821 sceptical navvies blasted St Patrick's Well off the map in the interests of a much more tangible Irish connection – a new harbour for the short sea crossing.

Northern Ireland is only 35km (22 miles) from Portpatrick and only the remote and inhospitable Mull of Kintyre offers a shorter sea journey from the British mainland. For centuries,

Portpatrick's little cove has sent out and received countless small craft crossing the North Channel between Scotland and Ireland.

The journey can be very rough and many craft have foundered in the crossing. The Atlantic sweeps round Ireland with thousands of miles of motion behind it and cyclonic weather brewed over the ocean hurls its storms across the channel. Fierce cross-currents sweep up and down the coast of the Rhins as the tide flows and ebbs through the Irish Sea and small craft can come to a standstill against wind and a 5-knot tide.

Despite this, Ireland looks very close on a clear day and the sea has its benign moods. In 1947, Tom Blower swam the North Channel from Donaghadee to Portpatrick in 15 hours 26 minutes and a number of swimmers have improved on this time since then.

Donaghadee has a long link with Portpatrick as it is the nearest port to Britain and trade has passed between these harbours for centuries. Both have declined in importance now, as larger more sheltered ports have taken over trade, despite being farther apart.

Portpatrick's first pier was built in 1774 to the design of John Smeaton. Over the next century Thomas Telford, and the John Rennies, father and son, were involved in improving the harbour, with limited success. Portpatrick's heydays as a port were over. The lighthouse was taken down and transported to Colombo in Ceylon. A smaller inner light continued until 1900 when it became redundant on the lighting of Killantringan Lighthouse to the north-west.

Since the days of St Patrick, multitudes have passed through the little port. Peter the Great is reputed to have slept here in 1698 on his way to Ireland. The composer, Franz Liszt, passed through in 1841. Soldiers, statesmen, refugees, farm workers and labourers have come and gone, horses, cattle and their attendants, and runaway couples – for Portpatrick was to Ireland what Gretna Green was to England. Scotland's easier marriage laws attracted amorous couples from both countries and hasty marriages were performed in Portpatrick as at Gretna before the pursuing parents arrived.

The military campaigns in Ireland made Portpatrick an important port for the British and, as coaching and postal services developed, it was natural for the Post Office to direct its mail this way. But the storms, dangers and inconveniences were exercising official minds in the mid-19th century and Holyhead, Greenock and Ardrossan were competing for business. The development of the sheltered harbour at

Stranraer settled the issue. The railway reached Stranraer in 1861 and Portpatrick in 1862. The railway still operates in Stranraer today, linking with the Irish ferries, but passenger services to Portpatrick ceased in 1950, three-quarters of a century after the Government abandoned its port. Apart from seamen's strikes, when Portpatrick has done brisk unofficial business in returning stranded travellers across the channel, it remains of minor use as a port for small fishing boats and pleasure craft.

The road into the village drops down Holm Street and Main Street, past the Dinvin Burn, to end opposite the harbour under a leading light on a lamp-post which is used to guide the lifeboat in after dark. To the left is the south pier with a jumble of rocks and the short, brick-faced lighthouse. To the right, the North Crescent leads round the harbour wall to the inner harbour where the Southern Upland Way starts. Car-parking spaces are abundant here as far as the toilet block, providing walkers with a comfortable send-off on their long journey. There is a wide choice of accommodation.

The Way takes off upwards, appropriately, by a good tarmac path between the tennis courts and the children's play-area. The path snakes uphill on the edge of the cliffs past the wide terrace taken up by the Portpatrick Hotel. This massive building pokes its conical turret-caps well above the harbour, dominating the village. It was designed by J. K. Hunter and built for Charles Orr Ewing, laird of Dunskey estate, between 1901 and 1905. Hunter also designed many of the brightly coloured Victorian houses and villas below. Houses crowd the slopes around the bay, with numerous windows looking down like spectators' eyes on an arena. The harbour is indeed an arena. It is the focal point for villagers and visiting tourists and the views to it from the hotel area are superb.

The lifeboat bobs at its mooring in the inner basin, awaiting its frequent calls out. A lifeboat has been stationed here since 1877. The line of the former railway and one of its bridges can be seen high above the harbour. Trains approached Portpatrick from the south and a deep cutting used by them is obvious on the skyline. The station sat on the east side of the village and is now a caravan site. A steep branch line led down to the harbour for a time but did not last long. The ruins of the 16th-century Dunskey Castle sit a short distance south of the village beyond the cutting.

The Way passes left of the hotel along the cliff-edge and looks into gullies and coves, while seagulls and fulmars wheel above the sea-pinks. The Southern Uplands is generally a region of smooth outlines with softly coloured vegetation masking the Silurian and Ordovician rocks. Here at its edge, though, sea and the elements have torn back the skin to reveal the underlying dark greywacke, a type of sandstone. The cliff-path is broad and firm but care is called for as it is easy to forget about the awful drops below in the excitement of enjoying the scenery. Extra care is required in windy weather when a sudden gust could sweep across the path. Both tourists and locals make use of the path with its wide views to Ireland and the Mull of Galloway. The 195m-high chimney of the Kilroot power station near Carrickfergus can be seen on Belfast Lough.

The high vantage point on the cliffs is used by British Telecom and HM Coastguard to maintain watch and links with shipping in the area. The Radio Station came under Post Office control in 1921 and has aerial masts 35 metres high. The Way goes around both establishments on the cliff-edge, then climbs some steps to a road which leads from a line of houses built for the coastguards in 1933. Turn left along the road, passing between a Ministry of Technology building with another aerial and Dunskey Golf Course. A gate leads upwards along the edge of the golf course over Cove Hill, which supports two of the big aerials.

The slope to the sea is easier now and gorse bushes and stonechats replace cliffs and seabirds. The wooded policies of Dunskey estate lie inland from the route.

The path continues left of the golf course, outside a line of white marker posts, dropping gradually down, then steeply as the path twists to Port Mora. This is known locally as Sandeel Bay and is a little cove with a grey sandy shore and some steep but not very high banks and cliffs to north and south. The path drops almost to sea-level at the south end and could be washed by high tides. There are caves in this corner called variously the Hermit's Cave, the Dupping Cave, and the Cave of Uchtriemackean. A burn splashes over the entrance to the smaller cave where, on the first night of May, it was the custom to bring those suffering from ailments to bathe in the water.

The burn and beach are easily crossed to the end of a dirt road. A few steps up this road a path doubles back left, up stone steps to traverse seawards by a terrace across the steep face of the flat-topped Islay Knoll. This leads round the corner to Port Kale or Laird's Bay which is much stonier than Port Mora. Here an attractive little grey and white building is designed on a double-hexagon plan under a tall red and yellow cable-marker pole. This is the landfall for a submarine telephone cable across the North Channel from Ireland. The first cable was laid in the 1850s. Near the Victorian Cable

House, a track leads off up Dunskey Glen while a bridge crosses the Dunskey Burn onto the stony beach.

The area is rich in natural history. Stonecrop and honeysuckle are abundant by the path, common storksbill flowers among the stones on the beach and bloody cranesbill makes a colourful show at the foot of the cliffs. Cross the beach to these intimidating cliffs and turn left towards the sea. Pass behind a large detached piece of cliff. Rise and fall on the path behind another detached piece of cliff and a steep staircase of steps with a chain handrail is revealed. Climb this and cross a stile at the top into sheep pasture.

The route continues west then north across easy grassy slopes, keeping height to avoid the ins and outs of the coastline but avoiding veering unnecessarily uphill. Portpatrick is well out of sight now and, with several kilometres clocked up, the Way-walker eagerly anticipates each change of scene, looking for the lighthouse at Black Head where the route swings inland.

The gully of March Howe cuts back into the hillside, causing some extra down and up work, but the best route across is easily recognised by the strengthening work done to the path. As Black Head is neared, a fence separates the route from the coastline.

In February 1982, the Cypriot-registered coaster *Craigantlet* left Belfast Lough for Liverpool but forgot to turn right and sailed 30 kilometres through the night to run on to the rocks directly under the light of Killantringan Lighthouse on Black Head. The deck cargo of containers was smashed up on the rocks of Portamaggie, the cove south of the lighthouse. Toxic waste had already leaked into the sea leading to emergency measures which included evacuating the lighthouse and keeping the public off the shore. However, the public have now been assured that no danger exists provided they keep inland from the fence.

Killantringan, as already mentioned, replaced the light on this coast at Portpatrick in 1900. It has a white tower of medium height on the top of the hill and a red foghorn lower down the slope. The gabled entrance porch to Killantringan bears the inscription 'In Salutem Omnium 1900'. The public are admitted to the lighthouse at the discretion of the keeper and a notice at the gate informs when it is open or closed.

The Way joins the road just below the lighthouse and turns right to follow it inland. The final view north along the coast is over the sands of Killantringan Bay below the slumped cliff-line to the House of Knock. Walkers may console themselves on the duller road-route with the knowledge that the coastline may be more scenic but it is about 3000km longer to

Killantringan Lighthouse and Portamaggie from the south

Cockburnspath that way!

There are several cattle grids along the road to prevent farm animals from straying. A walking boot placed at right angles to the bars is in no danger of slipping into the gaps but less confident walkers are apt to risk sprained ankles. Anyone lacking in technique should use the gates provided at the side.

The road climbs for several kilometres through farming land and passes the farm of Killantringan to emerge on the A764. Turn left along this road for about 400m, then take the minor road to the right just before a standing stone in a field. The farm road now being followed turns north as it climbs uphill, then north-east past one of several dwellings called Knock and Maize, to a Y-junction. Double back along the acute angle of the junction to the south, following the road as it turns east and downhill to cross a small burn, then climbing again on a rougher surface to a derelict house and steading. Pass left of the house along a track and through a gate to follow the right-hand side of a fence uphill through sheep and cattle grazings, to a viewpoint cairn specially built for the Southern Upland Way on Mulloch Hill.

There is a splendid view from here in all directions over the green, undulating Rhins to the wider horizons of Ireland, Kintyre and the Galloway Hills. Ailsa Craig is a sharp dramatic triangle to the north with the serrated ridges of Arran beyond. The ferry terminal and ship-breaking yard at Cairnryan stand out to the north-east, while the Merrick lords it over the Southern Uplands across the nearby Knockquhassen Reservoir. A prominent tower on Craigoch Hill to the north was erected in 1850 to Sir Andrew Agnew, the 7th Baronet of Lochnaw.

The Way bends in a right angle on Mulloch Hill and descends to the south-east to cross a fence and skirt Knockquhassen Reservoir some distance back on the south. The walk has a surprisingly rough moorland character now, with the sea hidden and heather underfoot. Gorse is thick around the south-east corner of the reservoir where the route crosses a fence to join the reservoir track by a concrete ruin south of Knockquhassen Farm.

Go right on the vehicle track with fenced pastures on your left. The road improves beyond a gate, though it stays narrow and requires alertness for the very infrequent traffic on the sharp bends. The route continues along the road, crossing the Crailloch Burn and dropping past Little Mark and Greenfield to cross the Piltanton Burn.

The old county of Wigtown was considered to be one of the flattest of the 33 counties of Scotland. Walkers may doubt that statement in this area! A band of millstone grit is crossed and the walker is hemmed in by pastures and arable fields in a rolling landscape. At each bend, when you expect to see Stranraer, another hill confronts you. The Piltanton Burn is less than 2km from Loch Ryan at Greenfield yet it has to travel another 20km before it reaches the sea at Luce Bay.

The Way follows the road up the steep slope to a T-junction at Hillside Piggeries. Turn right here across the slope and turn left at the next T-junction where the old military road comes in from Portpatrick. This was part of a route over 100 miles long, reconstructed in the 18th century between Sark Bridge on the English border and Portpatrick, with a view 'to open a speedy and certain communication between Great Britain and Ireland; especially with regard to the passage of Troops from one kingdom to the other whenever the exigency of Affairs may require it.' A short way east along this road and at last the view opens out to Stranraer below, and the Galloway Hills, Loch Ryan, Arran and Ailsa Craig.

Stranraer sits at the head of Loch Ryan, which has a fjord-like character at its mouth. Steep slopes plunge down to the water at the western end of the Southern Upland Fault-line –

which runs across the country in a south-west direction from Dunbar. The line through Loch Ryan to Luce Bay may represent the remnant of an ancient river valley. So much has been stripped from the surface of the earth through the ages that we can only speculate. The advance and retreat of glaciers over the area, the uplift caused by the removal of the weight of the ice-sheets in warmer times, and inundations by the sea have left a gigantic puzzle with few clues to work on.

The head of Loch Ryan is a rather muddy-looking beach with a long pier jutting out to deeper water. Stranraer is a rail and ferry terminal with both forms of transport meeting at the pier-head. Passengers disembark from the Sealink Ferries from Ireland onto the train in a short walk. Stranraer Town had its own railway station until 1966. Half-way up the east shore of the loch at Cairnryan are the competing ferries of the Townsend Thoresen group. For those in need of a longer walk, it is possible to link the Southern Upland Way with the Ulster Way, using the Stranraer ferry.

Loch Ryan played an important part in World War II as a naval and sea-plane base. Part of the Mulberry Harbour was built here and towed to Normandy for the Allied landing in Europe in 1944. Somewhat earlier, Queen Victoria enjoyed four nights here on the royal yacht, and seventeen centuries before that the Romans were exploring it. The loch was famous at one time for its oysters, whilst sea-angling, water-sports and ship-breaking are all part of its varied activities today.

The blackest day in the area's history was the 31st January 1953. On that morning the *Princess Victoria* left Stranraer for Larne with 127 passengers and 49 crew in a gale. Beyond the shelter of Loch Ryan the heavy seas stove in the stern doors of this car-ferry causing water to rush in and the ship to list. Despite heroic rescue attempts by Portpatrick and Donaghadee lifeboats, the destroyer *Contest* racing from Rothesay Bay, and four ships sailing from Belfast Lough, the visibility was so bad that no contact was made with the stricken ship for over four hours after the first SOS. By that time the ship had gone down and 134 people had perished. A monument on the shore-front at Stranraer commemorates the grim event.

Stranraer is the market town for the Rhins and much of the south-west. Accordingly it caters for those in need of a meal or a bed. Claverhouse used its old castle in the town centre as his base at the end of the 17th century while persecuting the Covenanters. The North West Castle Hotel was the former home of Sir John Ross, who explored the North-West Passage, and with James Clark Ross (his nephew) discovered the North Magnetic Pole.

Those wishing to break their journey, once on the old Portpatrick military road, have only a 2km (1 mile) descent by road to the town centre. The Way comes no nearer than this but turns south-east, still on a minor road past Ochtrelure. The straight road eventually turns to the left then right again. Do not turn right but go on downhill by a footpath to Spout Wells.

The view southward from this area extends over Luce Bay to Burrow Head and the Isle of Man. The Royal Air Force base at West Freugh sits above the Sands of Luce and sends up low-flying jet fighters which scream across the area, so be prepared! There has been an airfield at West Freugh since World War I days, when airships patrolled the North Channel from here to protect shipping from German U-boats.

Turn right along another minor road at the bungalow at Spout Wells and head east of south past Stanlane to the courtyard farm of Whiteleys, through a gap formerly bridged to carry the railway from Stranraer to Portpatrick. Turn left at the A77 and follow it back 100m towards Stranraer then turn right up a wide lane. Pass a hay-shed on your right and a slight rise shows you the pylons at Stranraer Harbour on the left with the U-shaped gap of Loch Ryan beyond. Five old war-time gun emplacements are passed in line with Loch Ryan. The brick and concrete structures project as bastions from a circle to cover all directions but would be mainly on the lookout for enemy aircraft approaching from the sea, along the line of the fleet anchorage in the loch.

Turn right along another minor road, then left at the next junction to head north-east again. The big plantation ahead to the left is part of Culhorn estate where the Earl of Stair employed William Adam in the early 18th century to alter his house and landscape the garden. Adam was himself a notable architect, but is best known for fathering the famous sons, Robert and James, who carried on the tradition.

Continue along the road, with smallholdings nearby making use of old war-time buildings. Cross the Black Stank Burn, which gives the illusion of flowing uphill, and pass larger fields to a T-junction in front of a wood. Go left here then right at a split, taking the upper track. Go right again at another junction with a high bank on your left and follow the deteriorating road across a clearing and into a more mature wood. Culhorn Loch is glimpsed through the trees on the left, then the roofline of Stranraer is seen again from a clearing. More woods lead back to a tarred road at a little stone lodge which has two centrally placed chimney stacks. Turn right along the road which is another part of the old military road.

The railway from Stranraer is on the left and Loch Ryan can be seen again. Pass an unmanned level-crossing to Aird Farm, where lived at 30 metres above sea-level the cousin of Sir Edmund Hillary, the conqueror of Everest. Unmanned railway crossings are fairly common features of the flat farming regions in Scotland but are rare in hilly areas, where the contortions of the landscape offer more bridge points.

The next road junction shows Loch Magillie to the south. Soulseat Loch just beyond it was the site of an abbey founded in the 12th century. Turn left under the railway bridge, which has an unusually low girder parapet, and almost immediately, turn off the road to the right to follow a path through a long plantation north of and parallel to the railway. This is the line which runs north to Girvan and Ayr, branching at Troon to Glasgow, or to Kilmarnock, Carlisle and London. The direct route from Stranraer through Galloway to Dumfries and Carlisle was closed in 1965.

There is a good mix of trees in the plantation, providing colour at most seasons. The path is firm and leads to the outskirts of Castle Kennedy village. Pass a row of council houses on your left and go round the last house on to the road past an electricity sub-station. Go east along the road past the school and oil depot to a T-junction. There is an interesting row of old estate cottages down the right fork and the old station building which now provides bed and breakfast. The Way take the left fork to the A75, sometimes called the London Road.

Those walking east to west should have little difficulty reversing the directions but care is required descending the cliffs at Port Kale. If a bulky rucksack is worn, the descent may be made easier by facing inwards. The chain handrail should overcome any problems.

Looking along the canal joining the White Loch to the Black Loch from the entrance bridge to Castle Kennedy Gardens

Inch

CASTLE KENNEDY—NEW LUCE

DISTANCE: 15½km (9½ miles) HEIGHT RANGE: 25–145m

Walkers are now heading into more sparsely populated country where they will have to solve their own problems. The walking is still fairly easy and the section short. However, accommodation is limited in New Luce and it is not on a bus route, although the post-bus calls six days a week from Glenluce. It generally leaves Glenluce about 10.00 and arrives at New Luce around mid-day. The route is accessible by car at a number of points. Much of the walking is done on tarred road or hard forest road. The forest section may be rather intimidating to those with little experience, but the route follows the major road through the forest for most of the way, with little scope for error until near the end.

Inch is a parish in the north-west of the former county of Wigtown. It was created a burgh of barony in the 17th century for the Viscount of Stair. Before that the chief landowners were the Kennedys, whose Castle Kennedy gives its name to the village being left behind.

From the village, cross the busy A75 to the entrance to Castle Kennedy Gardens. The A75 is the 'Euro-route' along which heavy transporters trundle between the Irish ferries and the English Channel and North Sea ferries to Europe. The Castle Kennedy Gardens are open to the public, with an admission charge. Details are given on a notice at the gate. However, the Southern Upland Way follows the main drive down to the White Loch, where Lochinch Castle is seen on the north bank and the remains of the old church of Inch and its cemetery on the west bank. Inch is another name for an island and the church take its name from Inch Crindil, standing offshore in the White Loch or Loch of Inch. The

The ruinous Castle Kennedy, accidentally burnt in 1716

modern church of Inch is some 800m (½ mile) to the south and in its burial ground are interred the captain and other officers who perished in the *Princess Victoria* disaster referred to earlier. The White Loch is frequented by a large flock of greylag geese, joined by other species in winter.

Our route follows the tarred drive along the east side of the White Loch to a bus park for the Gardens near the south end of the Black Loch. The Way turns to the right uphill here, while car and pedestrian access to the Gardens goes left through a gate and over a canal. Those with time and energy to spare might wish to take the chance to see the gardens and the two castles. The canal connects the White Loch to the Black Loch and is crossed by a picturesque bridge leading to the car park, toilets, garden centre, tea room and entrance to the formal gardens where the admission fee is paid.

Just inside the formal gardens stand the ruins of Castle Kennedy which was accidentally burned down in 1716. It had been built in 1607, probably as the successor to an earlier castle. The Kennedys of that day were a ruthless and greedy family whose power spread from Ayrshire to Galloway and is commemorated in a rhyme:

'Twixt Wigton and the town of Air
Portpatrick and the Cruives of Cree,
No man needs think for to bide there
Unless he court with Kennedie.'

The Black Loch and Heron Isle

John, Lord Kennedy, was appointed Keeper of the Manor Place and Loch of Inch in 1482. His descendant, John, 7th Earl of Cassillis, came into hard times in the 17th century through his support for the Covenanters and had to sell off his Wigtownshire estates. Castle Kennedy came eventually to the Dalrymples of Stair who were to play prominent roles in the country's affairs.

John Dalrymple became Lord Advocate of Scotland in 1687 and joint Secretary of State in 1691 and was heavily involved in bringing about the Glencoe massacre of 1692, when a force led by Campbell of Glenlyon, quartered in the village of Glencoe, slew some 40 of its MacDonald hosts. John Dalrymple was created the 1st Earl of Stair in 1703 and was appointed a commissioner in 1705 to arrange the Treaty of Union between Scotland and England.

It was his son, the 2nd Earl of Stair, who transformed the estate to much of its present plan. As British Ambassador to France he had been greatly impressed by the gardens at Versailles and he sought to create a showpiece of his own estate. The accidental burning down of his home may have given the impetus for reconstruction of his other residence at Culhorn. Castle Kennedy was never rebuilt but its gardens were re-landscaped, using the muscles and horses of the Royal Scots Greys and the Inniskilling Fusiliers. Such expedients were then available to military officers destined to become Field Marshals!

On the peninsula between the White and Black Lochs, a round pond and terraces and other landforms were created on which to base the fine gardens enjoyed by all today. At the start of the 19th century the gardens had become neglected, but the 8th Earl, on his succession in 1840, restored them. In 1867 the 10th Earl built the Scottish Baronial-style Lochinch Castle, to return the family home to the estate after a century and a half of absence.

George Borrow was a visitor to the estate in 1866 in his travels and described it as the 'most beautiful scene I ever saw'. Today, spring and early summer are the best seasons for a visit, when the azaleas, rhododendrons, magnolias, camellias and Chilean firebushes are at their most colourful. A country trail has been established, with numbered posts to guide visitors to the best features of the garden, including the century-old avenue of Monkey-puzzles, Pinetum, and the sunken garden at Lochinch Castle. The castle is the home of the present Earl and Countess of Stair and is not open to the public.

Returning to the bus-park at the entrance to the Gardens, we rejoin the Way as it climbs up the road eastwards between estate cottages. Looking back there is a fine view over the Black Loch to the Uplands beyond. The wooded Heron Isle is a crannog – an artificial island created by prehistoric man where he and his family might dwell surrounded by water in relative safety from hostile tribes and savage animals. The bare smaller island is a nesting site for a flock of raucous black-headed gulls. This is a species which has increased greatly in numbers through its adaptation to living off humans. Scavenging round rubbish tips and flapping down to gobble up meal scraps put out for smaller birds in back gardens, these gulls multiply in direct relation to the untidiness of man. As they increase, other species tend to disappear through being ejected from their nesting sites or starved at the end of the queue. The only feeder burn flowing into the lochs comes down the side of Sheuchan Hill into the Black Loch while the only outlet leaves the same loch at the north end heading for Loch Ryan.

A short distance eastwards along the estate road brings the Way through a fringe of woodland to the edge of the policies. Turn left along the public road, passing a lodge to reach farming land again. To the south is the kettle hole of Cults Loch. A kettle hole originates when an ice-sheet settles over the land and the stream running from higher up the glacier deposits gravel over the ice. The gravel insulates the ice from the melting process, giving it more weight than its surroundings and allowing it more time to attack the earth's crust in the daily rise and fall of temperature. Ultimately a depression is formed, all the ice melts and the gravel sinks into the water-filled hollow.

There is another crannog in Cults Loch. The area was probably once part of a raised beach and the escarpment of Chlenry Hill which the Way is now approaching was once probably a sea-cliff.

The till left behind by the glaciers has been smoothed and cultivated over the centuries by farmers, providing a handy level site for a war-time aerodrome to the south of the loch. Old hangars and Nissen huts still dot the landscape. The Nissen hut is named after its designer – Col. P. N. Nissen – and has been much used for work or military camps where accommodation is required quickly for large numbers of people. Its half-round shape copies the design of the Eskimo igloo, allowing storms to be diverted over it, but the vertical ends are more vulnerable.

The road is being followed in a north-easterly direction past a side road going left to Sheuchan. Just after this, the Way turns off the road to the right before it bends, to pass along a track in front of Chlenry cottages (or Balnab on some maps).

A road in on the left joins up with the track under banks of common cumfrey – a plant often used for curing sores – and both run on to Chlenry Farm over a bridge. The farmhouse and main complex of buildings are passed on your left as you go through a gate and head up a lane bounded by a hawthorn hedge and a young plantation of trees. The lane is brilliant with colour in summer, with red, white, blue and yellow flowers set off boldly against the greens, while the slope on the east is a blue mist of bluebells. At the end of the lane, the route follows the right-hand side of a gorse-fringed wall as it heads uphill across grazing land. As it passes over the brow of the hill, the route is channelled through the narrowing gap formed between two plantations and joins the public road beyond, at a stile about 200m east of a cottage. Walkers going west from the road should seek out two gates in the gap to ensure hitting the route to the valley.

East-bound travellers now follow the narrow, twisting road through a rough upland landscape where the ranging calls of the curlew, lapwing and redshank can accentuate the loneliness. After about 500m (1/3 mile) the walker leaves the

Chlenry from the north

public road again to the right to follow a forestry road across a field and cross a stile at the Bareagle Forest gate. This is the first state forest met on the eastward cross-country journey.

Sitka spruce and lodgepole pine are the dominant trees here. The upright leading shoot of the spruce tends to be long and thin while the uppermost shoot on a pine tends to end in a thick, tail-like little bush. Both the sitka and lodgepole were introduced to this country from North America and do well in the damp climate on our poor shallow soils and exposed situations. The sitka spruce is named after a town in Alaska, and is easily recognised by its sharp jagged needles and the bluish-grey under-foliage which contrasts with the dark green outer colour. The lodgepole pine is so-called from its use by the American Indians to support their tents or lodges. This pine is distinguished by its needles being in pairs about 4cm long, and its cones which are flattened and not pointed at the base. The cone scales have a small projecting prickle.

Look out also for a few blocks of corsican pine with much longer needles which show a characteristic twist, and noble fir near the first bends in the road. From a distance the noble fir is distinctive for its matted horizontal layering of foliage. The larch is the only cone-bearing tree here to lose its foliage in winter. In summer, it puts on a fresh light-green show of leaves, in bundles or tufts sprouting at intervals along the twigs.

The forester chooses his trees carefully to suit the type of soil and the climate. One species may be planted to grow quickly and smother competing vegetation such as heather, allowing another species to grow better than it would on its own.

The Forestry Commission has to plan 40 or 50 years ahead when it drains, ploughs and plants a hillside. In that time, intending markets may disappear and others arise. As coal mines close, fewer pit-props are needed. As the railways contract, fewer wooden sleepers are required, and concrete provides an alternative choice. As the public's demand for newspapers, magazines, books and wrapping paper grows, more wood pulp is required. Fashions change in house building and decorating, and chipboards and hardboards are developed. Forestry has to adapt to a constantly changing situation, with the disadvantage that the product takes decades to grow.

The general direction of the Way along the forest road is south-east for about 1½km (1 mile). It then turns east, ignoring a branch route to the south, and continues for about 2km (1½ miles) with only a few shallow bends. It then begins to twist and turn as it changes its general direction towards the north. At this point the route turns eastwards to follow a prominent forest ride for a short distance, through a mixture of heather and bracken, until it meets a stone wall. To the south-east of this point there is open hill land offering extensive views of the Water of Luce, Luce Bay, Glenluce Abbey, the Castle of Park, the Mull of Galloway and, on a clear day, the Isle of Man.

The Way then turns northwards to follow the stone wall along another ride and thereafter takes a sharp turn eastwards once more, to climb to Craig Fell. There are restricted views at this point towards Kilhern and the Galloway Hills. The route descends through this forest ride and enters a break between some larch trees and continues to fall steeply until it bends to the left at a plantation of western hemlock (easily identified by the irregular lengths of their needles), and drops to a flat embankment which it follows northwards through mixed woodland with glimpses of the nearby railway.

Descending gently to the Craig Burn, the Way crosses a footbridge and stile. It then passes through an attractive wooded area with prominent rock outcrops.

The route continues to follow a rough track northwards before crossing a stile over a fence into a strip of conifer plantation. A trail is taken through the plantation running from south to north and parallel to the railway line, before crossing a stile over a fence and a stone dyke. The Way skirts a field for a very short distance, and then crosses a stile and a bridge over the railway. Once this bridge is crossed the route falls gradually south-eastwards through open pasture and down a grassy bank to the Water of Luce.

The Water of Luce is crossed by a new suspension footbridge erected by the army in 1983. A meadow is crossed and the edge of the field followed north-eastwards to join the public road south of Cruise Farm. Pass the farm, and immediately turn off the road uphill on a track to the right at the north end of a plantation.

Trees are left behind as the slope flattens out and green pastures and gorse bushes give way to rougher upland scenery again. The track leads on north of east in a long, undeviating straight across a level but time-textured scene towards the distant Kilhern. Heather moors, improved pastures and bracken-encroached old inbys speak of past differences in the land-usage through the centuries. Sheep and cattle stand about the landscape, eyeing intruders suspiciously. Their ancestors might well have been herded off along this same track in droving days, ambling eastwards on a vast journey of no return by Dumfries and Carlisle to the markets in the south. Galloway cattle are now driven in cattle floats to the markets at Newton Stewart and Stranraer – but their end is just the same.

By the 16th century the Borderers and Gallovidians were turning their attention from stealing cattle to breeding them more intensively for the growing populations in the towns of England. As times became more peaceful, a great annual trade developed. Northern-bred beasts were herded southwards to feed the people of the expanding towns. Streams of cattle from the Islands and the Highlands, Ireland and Galloway, the Lothians and the Borders, converged on the routes to the south. Colonial expansion and the Napoleonic War brought a demand for salted beef for the navy, but this declined as the steam-ship became established followed by the introduction of the railway and refrigeration introduced on cargo ships.

Droving made a lasting impact on the landscape, though. People were on the move again and roads and bridges were going to have to be provided for them. A network of communications had spread itself into every glen and the prehistoric and Roman routes – which had been neglected in the Dark Ages – were being re-discovered, improved, or supplanted. The Southern Upland Way walker follows a long tradition.

Our eastward trek ends for the moment at Kilhern. The Way passes the door of the derelict building, going round to the left under a brick tower which once supported a water tank. Civilisation takes water for granted. A turn of the tap and it flows for us. In an upland farm like this, with few contours of the map to overlook it, water was valued much more highly. For many weeks in the year there would be too much, as the westerly winds swept in with rain-laden clouds, but in spring and early summer, warmer and drier air masses could dominate, drying out the burns and parching the grass. Then every drop became precious and drought and gravity had to be offset.

The westerlies brought the rain but the winds to be feared were the biting cold blasts of winter. Mature ash and red-barked scots pine form a sheltering crescent from north-east to south around the farm, against the polar and continental winds from the easterly direction.

Although deserted now, this area is rich in archaeological remains, and there is much evidence of former occupation. Cairns and hut circles abound on the hills and not far from Kilhern are the Caves of Kilhern – a long, chambered cairn in which eight burial cists were uncovered. A cist may be described as a coffin made out of stone slabs, but much shorter than a modern coffin as the dead were buried in a bent-knees position.

The track is followed north-west from Kilhern, right of a grass field which low-lighting can show is ridged from having been ploughed in the past. Beyond a gate the track twists across a small depression, then crosses to the east side of the dyke to come over the crest of the hill and down the right edge of a larch plantation past a small ruined building. Although it is a very common term in Scotland, it is worth noting that 'dyke' denotes a stone wall. This minor point is worth making, in the interests of walkers less familiar with our language, as the word will recur many times throughout this Guide!

The descent commands a very good view over the valley of the Cross Water of Luce and up to Balmurrie on the first part of the next section of the Way. Beyond Balmurrie lie the real uplands of the south-west, and walkers can sense that the game is getting much more serious from here on. Dotted about the foreground are large heaps of stones gathered from the fields, illustrating the problems left by the glaciers to the first farmers.

The descent to the valley follows the track from the plantation and meets up with the road to New Luce about 2km (1 mile) east of the village. The larger village of Glenluce lies some 8km (5 miles) off the route to the south, whilst New Luce itself offers some possibilities of accommodation. It is the last community of any size before Glen Trool. There is guest-house and farmhouse accommodation. Walkers going west along the Way will find the track to Kilhern starting just west of a quarry, near to the waterfall on the Cross Water of Luce.

Cross Water of Luce

The Moors

NEW LUCE—BARGRENNAN

DISTANCE: 28km (17½ miles) HEIGHT RANGE: 45–250m

The crossing of this long section is a serious undertaking and should not be attempted by the inexperienced. The terrain is very bleak and confusing in places and there is ample scope for going astray. The area is sparsely populated and has few services at either end.

The section includes lengthy stretches of public road so a car can be used to shorten distances between New Luce and Balmurrie, and Derry and Bargrennan. Other walking conditions vary from forest roads, rides and farm tracks to rough moorland grass and heather paths. Low-lying parts of the moors can be alarmingly wet so stay on the route!

Special dangers to guard against are mist and inclement weather, and straying from the path on the moors and in the forest. The route demands some map-reading and compass skill as there are few features of distinction in the landscape. In good visibility it should be simple enough to follow the trail and waymarking posts, but any walker losing the route could be in serious trouble in bad weather. The problems are enhanced by the lack of shelter or transport on the route. Consideration should always be given to the effects of weather and the possibility that walkers might have to stay wet and cold for a long period. Public transport at either end consists of a post-bus once a day from Glenluce to New Luce (Mon.-Sat.) and a seven-day service from Newton Stewart via Bargrennan to Ayr three times a day (twice on Sundays).

The old county of Wigtownshire was divided into three sections – the Rhins, the Machars and the Moors. We have already met the Rhins, and seen the Machars stretching southwards into the Irish Sea to Burrow Head. Now we are facing up to the Moors in the most sparsely populated area of the old county and new district.

New Luce is a small village with one shop, a pub, and a church. Passenger trains haven't stopped at its station since 1965.

Alexander Peden, the notable Covenanter, was minister of the church from 1659–62 until he was ousted by the authorities and adopted a wandering ministry in constant danger from the dragoons. Despite confinement on the Bass Rock and being put on a slave-ship for America, 'Peden the Prophet' managed to end his days in his brother's house in Scotland. The parish church was built about 1821.

Old Luce parish contains the village of Glenluce 8km (5 miles) to the south. It is on a bus route and has a greater variety of services than New Luce. Glenluce Abbey is a Cistercian ruin in the care of the Department of the Environment. It is reported that lepers who gathered at Glenluce Abbey, were given a burial service and led on to the 'lepers trail', probably to the leper colony at Liberland, and that the lepers washed themselves in the Purgatory Burn and at the Wells of the Rees. The nearby 16th-century Castle of Park was built using stones from the abbey. Two notable Borderers to be met later on in the walk have connections here. Michael Scott the Wizard is said to have lived at Glenluce Abbey in the 13th century and Carscreugh Castle was the home of 'The Bride of Lammermoor', the tragic heroine of Sir Walter Scott's novel.

This section starts where the last left off – 2km (1 mile) east of New Luce and beyond Hardcroft on the minor road south of the Cross Water of Luce where the track comes north from Kilhern. The Way turns on to the road at an acute angle and follows it east then north-east, passing an iron footbridge which leads across the river. It is worth a few extra steps across the dyke here to see the attractive waterfall and gorge called the Loups of Barnshangan, with the river flowing black and deep beneath the bridge. A short way along the road again and we come to Dranigower Bridge with another attractive view of a much more open kind. Dranigower is off to the right but the Way and road carry straight on climbing towards Balmurrie.

The ditch banks on this stretch are vivid in spring and summer with the colour of primrose, violet, wood anemone, herb robert and other plants leading the eye upwards to gorse and hawthorn blossom. It is a remarkably rich and colourful rural scene, giving no hint of the abrupt transition waiting beyond Balmurrie.

As height is gained the land-use variations become more prominent, with shelter-belts of deciduous trees, conifer plantations, improved pastures and rough grazings dotted with farms, sheep and cattle. Just before Balmurrie, in the field to the left of the road, there is a good example of a lunky or smout – a hole built into the bottom of a dyke, just big enough for one sheep to pass through at a time. Farmers can board these holes up or open them to control the distribution of their flocks. Sometimes they may wish the sheep to graze with cattle in the next field whilst at other times it may be policy to separate them.

Balmurrie marks the end of the public road. It has an attractive garden shielded by swaying trees at this exposed site. The Way follows the rough track round the left side of the farm buildings, where the walker is immediately confronted by a different world – a wide, rough and treeless country leading into the unknown, as the route still climbs. The track and telephone poles go off left to Kilmacfadzean at the edge of 20th-century civilisation. The Way itself goes straight on left of sheep pens and a grey building, crosses to the right of the dyke, and heads northwards to cross the dyke again and cut diagonally across a pasture to leave the field near its north-east corner beside a smaller stone-walled enclosure.

The prominent Carn na Gath to the east is a good route-marker at this stage. It is a much altered cairn of ancient date. A land-rover track is followed northwards over the hill from the top of the field and the Moors are now revealed in their wildness, stretching to the afforested heights beyond. It is advisable to study the map carefully at this point, to identify the main landmarks of a rather featureless area. Walkers who blunder on regardless are asking for trouble – and bewilderment once the route has been lost.

Far to the north are three distinct hills – the one on the right being lower than the other two but more sharply peaked. Craigairie Fell in the middle is the highest hill in the district and is the walker's target. To the north-west is an area of high ground rising to the lumpy and undistinguished Quarter Fell, Big Craigenlee and White Fell. To the east is the prominent Artfield Fell, with the lower Balmurrie Fell in front, and Eldrig Fell coming into view behind these two ridges.

To keep to the correct path, the walker should continue northwards – into ground which is due to be planted with trees from 1984 onwards – over a fence at the right-hand end of a section of chest-high dyke (after a gap, the broken dyke continues at knee height). Drainage ditches lead from here to the crossing point on the Mulniegarroch or Purgatory Burn – which is insignificant in size despite its grandiose title. The Way now goes left of a dyke and follows the drier ridge northwards with some unexpected rock outcrops to the west, and two prominent cairns to the south-west on the horizon.

With the Purgatory Burn behind on your left and the Tarf Water well to your right you are now on course to come to a gate in a fence, so long as you stay high. Straying off the ridge will only lead you into wet morasses, especially along the Tarf. The gate in the fence is a key feature. Anyone not finding it is advised, as in the game of 'Monopoly', to return to 'Go' and start again – or at least to return to the last recognisable feature.

Still heading for Craigairie Fell and its forest you should now be seeing the inbys of Laggangarn, where grass worthy of a bowling green stands out in startling contrast to the paler moor grasses and darker heaths. The Way drops down a little burn past the ruins of Laggangarn and a solitary wide-spreading tree, then up again to two standing stones and an ancient monuments sign. The Standing Stones of Laggangarn are two early Christian memorial stones dating from about the 8th century. Both stones have an incised cross on their southern sides and four smaller simpler crosses – one in each of the angles of the larger cross. The area is the site of a now-deserted settlement although sheep are still pastured on the grass.

From Laggangarn we look northwards into Killgallioch Forest. The ruined farm of Killgallioch can be seen among the trees to the north-east. Just north of the standing stones is the Tarf Water – the main stream draining this basin. The Tarf is normally just a small burn at this point but a bridge has been provided to allow for its turbulent moods after rain.

After the crossing, the Way enters an established forestry plantation and goes uphill by a rough firebreak with a broken-down dyke on the right for guidance. Yellow signs with white arrows point back to the south-west to guide forest-walkers to the standing stones. Beyond them, Way-walkers going west should seek out the route markers of Laggangarn settlement ruins, the dry ridge above leading to the gate in the fence, the dyke on the left leading to the crossing-point on the Purgatory Burn, and the chest-high section of dyke running across the route which leads to Carn na Gath and Balmurrie.

Walkers heading for the east through Killgallioch Forest should remember to travel against the direction of the arrow posts as they follow the ride for 70m up from the Tarf Water and veer to the right on the shoulder of Craigairie Fell. Stay with the dyke (no longer ruinous) going uphill as it crosses other rides.

As the slope eases off, a sign is met pointing the direction back to the Laggangarn Stones and down to the 'Wells o' the Rees'. The Wells are a few minutes walk off the Way but are well worth visiting. A ree is another name for a sheepfold and various dyked enclosures vie for attention so that the Wells are not obvious at first, but another sign stands above them and marks the site in a clearing.

The Standing Stones of Laggangarn

There are three wells where water seeps out of the ground, with a dome of unmortared stones built over each. The structures are of considerable age and are probably of religious significance as a chapel and graveyard once stood here. The clearing in the forest has an open prospect to the south and the view on its own is worth the visit.

Back on the Way again at the upper sign to the wells, the dyke has vanished, but at Creag-dhu a tall and very prominent cairn leads onwards to the end of a ride running across the slope now. The cairn is another good viewpoint and looks ahead over Loch Ochiltree to the big hills around Glen Trool, and back to the lonely Moors and rolling farmlands of the Rhins. Rough little hills projecting from the Moors assume a stature well beyond their true measure.

In the middle distance, the red corrugated iron house at High Eldrig sits alone and remote beside its loch under Eldrig Fell.

The sea looks a long way off in Luce Bay and Wigtown Bay, and the Southern Upland Way is now well into the uplands – but the real heights have still to come farther east. The Creag-dhu cairn is left behind, the corner turned, and the firebreak followed on, contouring across the east side of Craigairie Fell to join the forest road at a meeting point of three signposted routes – Kilgallioch road north, Kilgallioch road south, and Kilgallioch road east. The Way enters from the south road and turns an acute angle to take the east road past a sign pointing back to the Wells o' the Rees and Laggangarn Stones.

As the road is followed south-eastwards at first, before turning to the east, sharp-eyed walkers can scan the northern slopes of Craigmoddie Fell ahead for Linn's tomb. Four grey stone walls make a box-like shape around the grave of Alex Linn among the outcrops below the summit. He was a Covenanter martyr shot at this place in 1685 by Lieutenant-General Drumond during the 'Killing Time'. The grave has been restored on several occasions, with solemn commemoration services attended by sizeable groups of worshippers. Several trees by the tomb have been cut down and replaced by a hawthorn, now protected by a fence. The tomb lies about 1km (½ mile) south of the Way and can be visited from where the Way runs along the edge of the forest. A gate here leads on to the ridge at the best approach.

Back on the Way, the forest road continues eastwards through sitka spruce and lodgepole pine and across a clearing. This leads north to the kettle hole lake of Loch Derry which can be seen by taking a few extra steps to the left. About 2km to the north of Loch Derry there was once a leper colony at

Craigairie Fell from Linn's Tomb

Liberland. The road leads on, with more clearings punctuating the end of the forest, and Derry Farm is seen below with the next section of the route a straightforward road walk.

The forest road curls down to pass left of the farm at a gate and sign advertising Linn's Tomb, Wells o' the Rees, and Laggangarn Stones. Derry is a Blackfaced sheep-breeding farm but Belted Galloway cattle are conspicuous in neighbouring pastures. The Belted Galloway is a handsome beast, normally coloured black save for a broad white band round its middle between the shoulders and the hips. It is bred for its beef and can survive out of doors on rough grazings in south-west Scotland where the weather tends to be less harsh than in many other parts of the country.

The Way follows the farm road from Derry, becoming better surfaced farther east as it becomes public. Farmland gradually gives way again to state and private forest beyond Polbae, where the Polbae Burn flows around an area of blanket bog before passing under Darloskine Bridge. The road and Way turn sharply to the right across this bridge at a derelict little lodge. Polbae House dates from 1879 and sits amidst some splendid amenity planting which is much enjoyed by the bird-life. There is another herd of Belted Galloways at Polbae and a tall slim cairn on a hillock in a plantation just south of the road. The pitted granite inscription is just decipherable as 'M.S.Fox 1913'. Marmaduke Septimus Fox celebrated his 21st birthday in 1913 and this cairn was built to commemorate the event at Polbae, where the family lived.

Beyond Tannylaggie the road crosses the River Bladnoch by a stone bridge and passes Waterside which keeps a flock of brown-woolled Shetland sheep. The road returns to the Bladnoch, now increasing in size and depth as it meanders off to Wigtown Bay, whilst the Way climbs through Waterside Forest to join the B7027 from Barrhill to Newton Stewart. Turn right along this minor road to the nearby hamlet of Knowe. A ruined house on the right carries the date 1856 and curled skewputts (the lowest stones of the gable coping), but the lived-in dwelling on its right is ten years or so older and was once the Snap Inn. The ruined school across the road by the phone box still has a hitching ring on the wall for tethering horses. Under a beech tree behind the school are the ruins of a water-powered mill. The fertile drumlins in this area which once produced crops are now disappearing under forests.

Knowe is a quiet residential area occupied by two or three families, and traffic on the road is scarce. Yet the evidence shows that this hamlet was once the centre of a much more populated neighbourhood before the drift to the town began and the mill, inn and school closed down. For those who live here the car at the door is an essential link with the outside world, for public transport is non-existent.

The bridge over the Beoch Burn at the end of the hamlet carries a 1933 datestone and an Ordnance Survey benchmark. Benchmarks take the form of a crow's foot on a level line incised into an immovable object, such as the mortared stonework on a bridge or building. From it, the map-maker can survey the surrounding landscape and map the variations in levels using this mark as a datum.

Cross the bridge and immediately turn off the road to the left to follow a line of rides through the Penninghame Forest in a north-easterly direction. This climbs gradually along the edge of a low ridge with views to the west, then emerges from the forest eastwards on to a minor road to Bargrennan at Glenruther Lodge, where a line of tall beech trees cast a moment of shade over the now open route.

We are back to a rough moorland character hilltop again going northwards past Glenruther Farm before leaving the road at a cattle grid under the Hill of Ochiltree as the road turns to the left. The Way goes on up to the north-east crossing a shallow depression on the slope which is part of the De'il's Dyke. It is a common custom in Scotland to attribute things to the Devil if they cannot be otherwise explained. This dyke is an ancient earthwork of unknown origin which is thought to have run from Loch Ryan to the Solway Firth. Whether it was meant for defence or as a territorial boundary is a matter for speculation. Joseph Train, the antiquarian friend of Sir Walter Scott, was an early Southern Uplands walker, tracing the dyke from end to end. It would be very difficult to do this today as there is so little to see and part of the route has been planted with trees.

The summit of the Hill of Ochiltree is visited next, just a short distance above the De'il's Dyke. Though only 170m high, the hill is surrounded by lower ground, except for its near neighbour Glenvernoch Fell, giving it wide views in all directions. Loch Ochiltree spreads itself west of the hill – a glacially impounded loch in an undulating landscape of smaller lochs and morainic debris. The Loch of Fyntalloch fills a hollow in the boulder clay beside its bigger neighbour and drains into it. The ridge to the west of Loch Ochiltree shows a crag and tail outline where harder resistant rock has stood firm against the advancing ice sheets, which have passed by to smooth out the contours behind. Green and fertile drumlins roll above the heather-clad peaty moors and mosses.

Tree-clad islands on the loch show how the landscape once looked before sheep and deer destroyed the natural regeneration of forest cover in a slow campaign of genocide. Tender, infant trees make a juicy morsel to hungry animals, and as sheep and deer numbers have increased so the tree numbers have declined. As man killed off the red deer's natural predators and began to husband sheep intensively, their numbers increased dramatically and the natural regeneration of the woodland ceased. Mature trees stood unharmed for a while in their glory but, as they died off, there were fewer and fewer replacements growing to take their places. Man also cleared woodlands for fuel, or bark, used in tanning hides. Now the pattern has been reversed with a vengeance. As we look to the east we see the massive Galloway Forest Park dominating the countryside.

Glen Trool lies straight ahead like a great throat in the hills. To its left the slopes sweep up over the Fell of Eschoncan, Bennan Hill, and Benyellary (the hill of the eagle) to Merrick – or The Merrick as it is known in the south-west – the 844m (2770 feet) dominant point of Galloway, and indeed it is the highest hill in the Southern Uplands. The range it commands points its finger ridges westwards, giving the hill-mass its unusual name – the Awful Hand. The three northern summits of Shalloch on Minnoch, Tarfessock, and Kirriereoch give their names to farms at the foot of their ridges, but farming has contracted here as the great spruce forests have spread like a skirt round the base of the hills and well up the slopes.

Glentrool village can be seen peeping from the trees beyond the caravan site at Bargrennan. The forest village was created in 1953 to house the community of forestry workers planting and tending one of the largest forests in Scotland. Some of the houses in the village are available for let and can make useful bases for exploring this magnificent hill area. To the east and south, Ochiltree Hill looks along the valley of the River Cree where the Forestry Commission plantings are softened by fringes of alder and clumps of birch and oakwoods. The Lamachan range of hills rises high to the south of Glen Trool, then comes the gap between Newton Stewart and New Galloway and the ground rises again to the level granite summit of Cairnsmore of Fleet – just off the route map, south of the very scenic A712 tourist route – and the lower coastal hills at Creetown, decorated with masts and aerials.

The Cree estuary is conspicuous to the south-east, with the martyrs monument on Windy Hill at Wigtown visible in clear air high above its west bank. The obelisk erected 'to all martyrs' commemorates in particular Margaret Wilson and Margaret McLauchlan (aged 18 and 63) who were tied to stakes at the mouth of the River Bladnoch at Wigtown and drowned by the rising tide for their Covenanting beliefs. Margaret Wilson came from Glenvernoch 2km (1 mile) north-east of the Hill of Ochiltree, which we leave now in a northerly direction to rejoin the road which has detoured to the west round the hill. The road is followed north-east then east to Garchew, losing height as it heads into the Cree valley. Oak and birch dot the northern slopes of Glenvernoch Fell on the right. Just past Garchew, the Way crosses a dyke and goes left through the fields on the south side of the burn and rises amongst the grassed-over bulges of a moraine to drop down to the A714 Girvan-Newton Stewart road at Bridgend Cottage and cross the Middle Bridge of Cree at the hamlet of Bargrennan.

The Galloway Hills

BARGRENNAN—ST JOHN'S TOWN OF DALRY

DISTANCE: 38½km (24 miles) HEIGHT RANGE: 45–320m

The walking gets longer and the altitude higher, but there is a bus route at both ends. Dalry has a range of services and there is limited accommodation around Bargrennan. The bothy at White Laggan (NX 467775) is very useful but can be busy at times. Bothies at Culsharg (NX 415821) and Backhill of Bush (NX 481843) could also be used but are off the route. The Forestry Commission's camp site at the Caldons is on the route and can be thoroughly recommended. Walkers need to plan accommodation ahead on this lengthy stretch of the Way. Cars can reach the route in a number of places except in the middle section between Loch Trool and Clatteringshaws Loch. The Way takes on a distinct change of character in this section. Much of it is within the Galloway Forest Park, with high hills and rugged scenery, a beautiful loch and river for company, impressive woodland and forest stretches, historical associations and very interesting wildlife. Red deer, roe deer and wild goats inhabit the area and birds of prey are sometimes seen. Glen Trool is a major tourist attraction, and those not fit enough for the whole of this stretch of the walk can still enjoy it in parts with the aid of a car. Glentrool village, 2km off the route, has a shop. Newton Stewart is the tourist centre for the area and has a wide range of services. The Newton Stewart to Ayr bus passes through Bargrennan and calls at Glentrool village (seven days). The Ayr to Dalry and Castle Douglas route has a six-day service. Barrhill (15km or 9 miles from Bargrennan) has a midnight train to Stranraer for those desperate to escape from the route! The plot of Dorothy L. Sayers' detective story *The Five Red Herrings* hinges on a desperate cycle run from Bargrennan to Barrhill to catch a train.

The section starts at the Middle Bridge of Cree at Bargrennan. The hamlet is so scattered and hidden by trees from here that it seems to consist only of one house and a village hall. However, the church is not far behind the hall and there is more of the place beyond the fork in the road. The Way itself leaves the A714 opposite the hall and takes to the east into the forest by a firebreak. This break curves northwards, parallel to the road and the sound of the traffic, until it meets the main west to east ride. There is a good view from the junction over the House o' the Hill and Garlies Lodge to Glencaird Hill, then the main ride is followed eastwards rising over the 120m Rig of the Cairn.

Lamachan and Larg Hill rise in the east above the forests with the ride making straight for them. In summer the ride is at present a jungle of tall bracken, bog myrtle, heather and coarse grasses but will become much easier as the route is used. A broken wall and a ruined fence run down the ride and should be kept on your right. After about 1km (½ mile) a T-junction is met and the route taken by the wall to the north, curving east and ignoring a fork to the left. Mulldonoch and Lamachan Hill are now ahead as the Way crosses another T-junction and drops, with a burn on the right, to the minor road from Clauchaneasy to Glen Trool.

There is a large open space at this point where cars can be parked, and an outcrop of rock on the west side of the road to mark the entry point to the forest for those heading for Bargrennan. Eastbound walkers cross the road, following the trail north of the burn through a short stretch of mixed woodland until a stile leads into the corner of a field. Go left here and join up with the vehicle track which leads to a bridge over the river in an area of gravel workings and some recreational use. There is a scout hut just beyond the bridge.

The river is the Water of Minnoch and the east bank is now followed northwards through very attractive scenery of dividing channels, deep pools, stony shallows, flood-resisting levees, natural woodlands and open spaces – with the Galloway hills promising more variety ahead.

As the river is followed upstream, the junction is reached with the Water of Trool. The Minnoch appears as the smaller river here as it emerges from the forest in a narrow cutting. The Trool is more open and wider-looking but it is the tributary of the much-longer Minnoch.

The Way turns to the east now, along the south bank of the Water of Trool. Beyond a waterfall we come to a split channel and two bridges built by the Royal Engineers in 1970. These offer escape from the Way to the Glen Trool road, along a Forestry Commission walk to Stroan Bridge on the Minnoch.

The Stroan Bridge Walk now links up with the Southern Upland Way at the Engineers Bridge and both run together eastwards along the south bank of the Water of Trool.

A hiccup in its course gives a slight detour round the stretch of river known as the Black Loup but the extra distance is repaid in summer with yellow water lilies, and views over the water to the hills on both sides of the glen. The greyish-white streaks of the intrusive granite of the central core of the hills show up well from here amidst the rounded whalebacks of sediments of lower Palaeozoic age with their thin coats of vegetation.

From Jenny's Burn onward the riverside becomes more wooded as the path twists among moraine heaps. This is the Caldons Wood which survived a serious fire in 1978 when the new plantations to the south were devastated as an east wind swept a fire down the glen. The fire had been started by a careless human. Thousands of pounds of damage was done and numerous birds and animals destroyed in an area which is only now beginning to recover.

The fire started at the stile, near a notice reading 'Stroan Bridge 2¼ miles'. A short concrete path at right angles to the Way leads from here to a stone enclosure and the Martyrs Tomb. The monument commemorates six Covenanters, surprised here at prayer by Colonel Douglas, Lieutenant Livingston, and Cornet James Douglas 'and by them most impiously and cruelly murthered for their adherence to Scotlands Reformation Covenants National and Solemn League 1685'. An 1827 granite tablet is built into the wall around the sandstone gravestone, which is said to have been the first one renovated by Old Mortality. Sir Walter Scott's novel *Old Mortality* was written in admiration of the Cameronian stone-mason, Robert Paterson, who devoted the last forty years of his life to restoring this and other gravestones of Covenanting martyrs.

The route continues east to the Forestry Commission's very pleasant Caldons caravan and camping site at the south-west end of Loch Trool. The site is open from April 1-Sept. 30 and includes a shop, hot showers, and clothes-drying cabinets – which can work wonders for a long-distance walker's morale. Pitches are sited informally among the oak, birch, hazel and alder surroundings, which give the site a quality far removed from those where caravans are ranked side by side in close formation.

The Way skirts round the south side of the site, passing south of Caldons House and following up the south bank of the Caldons Burn to a forest road. Go left along this, with the view opening out north-eastwards to the Fell of Eschoncan

The Martyrs' Tomb in the Caldons Wood

and Buchan Hill. This leads to the Forestry Commission's trail across the southern slopes of Loch Trool. The area contains several paths established by the Forestry Commission which are much used from the camp site, so any unfamiliar direction posts may be fairly confidently relied on to lead to the route south of the loch or else back to the camp site. The Way and the Forest Trail travel together to a maximum height of about 160m, south of the loch, sharing some magnificent views over the loch.

Benyellary to the north stands out boldly above its corries up the valley of the Buchan Burn – a hanging valley which sends its burn cascading through the oakwoods in white cataracts down to Loch Trool. The rocky Fell of Eschoncan stands to its left, having resisted the glaciers which sheared off the valley sides and over-deepened the valley floor. Green pastures of improved land skirt the lower slopes, with invasions of bracken here and there, and a sinuous head-dyke hangs precariously on the slopes below dark summits of rock and heather. In front of the Fell sits the Bruce's Stone – a massive boulder commemorating the victory by King Robert the Bruce in 1307 over an English force. There is a large car-park near the stone at the end of the public road, providing good picnic sites and a popular base for hill-walking excursions. The easiest ascent route to the Merrick starts here.

The Gairland Burn topples out of another hanging valley to run into the north-eastern corner of the loch, slowing as it levels out, and infilling the loch-end with its sediments in an extensive delta. Under certain lighting conditions a tongue of alluvium can be seen under the water, spreading out into the middle of the loch from the extended banks of the burn. These banks have been broken through at an S-shaped bend giving the burn two routes into the loch now.

The routes up the Buchan and Gairland burns feature in S. R. Crockett's novel *The Raiders* – a thrilling blood-and-thunder tale played out in the granite heart of these hills.

The path along the south banks of the loch is quite rugged in places and requires some boulder-hopping as it threads through the forest. The steep slopes of Mulldonoch rise above the trees on the right and walkers can imagine for themselves the horrific scene in 1307 when according to tradition, as Sir Aymer de Vallance, the Earl of Pembroke, led his English force along the path in pursuit of Robert the Bruce, an avalanche of boulders descended upon them, followed by the Scots guerrilla band, in a successful ambush that turned the tide for Bruce. The Earl had been hoping to finish off his victory, achieved at Methven the previous year, when Bruce had narrowly escaped capture. Since then King Robert had been a hunted man, down on his luck – his young brother executed, his wife imprisoned, and he himself excommunicated by the Pope. From this time comes the famous legend of the spider in the cave, when the weary monarch is said to have watched the tiny creature try, try and try again in its efforts to pendulum over a gap and complete its web. And so he also tried again, returning to the mainland from exile and gathering his forces for another endeavour – and at Glen Trool his luck changed. In the same year, his old adversary Edward I of England died, and the succeeding Edward II had less fondness for foreign adventures. Gradually the English forces were ejected from Scotland until, in 1314 at Bannockburn, Bruce won for Scotland its independence.

Glen Trool Lodge sits on the north side of the loch near

Loch Trool at its west end

where it narrows in the middle. It is easily missed among the tall trees but it is of interest to many from its ownership by the Moores family of Littlewoods Football Pools. Employees of the firm often take a break here.

As the path nears the south-east corner of Loch Trool, it loses height and descends to the meadows east of the loch. Here it follows a dyke at the edge of the forest down to the Glenhead Burn where the Forestry Commission's trail returns to Buchan north of Loch Trool over a new footbridge. The route continues south-east along the south bank of the Glenhead Burn and then diverts southwards to follow up the Sheil Burn for a short distance, to meet up with a newly constructed forest road. The road climbs out of the plantation and heads steadily towards Loch Dee which lies over the crest. The Glenhead Burn and the road are heading for the same point – the col between Loch Trool and Loch Dee. Low-flying aircraft pilots frequently test their reactions at the same point, twisting out of one narrowing glen into the next. Some have paid the penalty for mistakes and have joined the toll of wrecked aircraft in these bewildering heights. Even an airship came to grief in 1917 on the back of Larg Hill which rises south of Glen Trool.

The views are restricted but attractive as the valley nears its head, with steep and impressive slopes on the south and the mysterious plateau containing the two hidden lochs of Glenhead to the north. Almost at the col the headwaters of the Glenhead Burn are diverted by dam to flow eastwards into the Dargall Lane and the catchment of Loch Dee.

Those going east follow the forest road now, with Loch Dee below on the left showing a little islet with a few scattered trees. As the road loses height Benyellary disappears behind and the south end of the Rhins of Kells takes increasing shape beyond Loch Dee. Bleached white granite boulders sit bulldozed aside by the road, where the road-makers shifted them out of their line of advance across the dark peat. Duller stones are scattered over the slopes where the ice-sheets left them. By the edge of the road, banks of glacial drift lie exposed under their top coating of heather, moor grass and peat.

To the left, Craiglee appears smooth and even-sloped until its summit ridge is studied. A more rugged and noble little hill would be hard to find in southern Scotland. As it is passed, its ribs begin to show and the 'even' slopes take on a more seamed and gullied aspect and something of the intricate geography of the hill becomes more evident.

Loch Dee expanding below shows a shore of white granitic sand and the ruins of a boathouse at the west end. The U-shaped valley of the Cooran Lane lies to the left, with the little slope to the valley floor causing extensive blanket-bog formation – now being drained to some extent by new plantations. Forests are normally planted below 400m but on the Kells they rise to 600m. The drainage from two of the lochs of the Dungeon, under the escarpment of Craignaw and the Cooran Buttress of Dungeon Hill, link up with the streams gullying the flanks of Corserine to form the headwaters of the River Dee, though it does not assume that title until the outlet at Loch Dee. Then the Black Water of Dee, to give it its more dramatic name, becomes a formidable river, tumbling out of the hills by the gap to the east through which the Way will shortly be heading. Before that, though, the Way has to turn south with the road away from Loch Dee to loop its way across the White Laggan Burn.

The White Laggan Bothy is a former shooting lodge and dwelling to the south-west of the bridge. After falling into ruin it was renovated by the Mountain Bothies Association and reopened in 1973. It has an unlocked door and is available for use to any passer-by, provided they respect the spirit and

Craiglee and Loch Dee from the White Laggan Bothy

intentions of its provision.

Returning to the bridge and the forest road back to Loch Dee, the Way passes to the left of the ruins of the Black Laggan and its complicated maze of in-by dykes. The three tall ash trees have seeded their heirs up the burn behind, now that the sheep flocks have been removed. The Black Laggan functioned as a herd's house after the White Laggan fell into disuse. Now the position is reversed – the Black Laggan is a derelict roofless shell and the White Laggan is a sound and often-occupied refuge. Enjoy its spectacular setting under the steep cleft in Curleywee and notice also the dark couloir on Millfore on the other side of the glen ere you turn north-eastwards out of the valley. A branch of the road comes in later on the right but the way forward is simple for a good stretch now.

As the corner of the Dee Valley is turned, the Merrick, then Benyellary appear in the Craiglee – Snibe Hill gap. The road runs parallel to the Dee until nearly opposite a large quarry on the far bank, then the Way takes the left branch of the road down to a concrete bridge over the river. The right branch runs to the public road at Craigencallie.

Once over the River Dee, the forest road forks left into the heart of the hills, and right to follow the Dee downstream. The Way takes the route to the right under the steep slopes of Darrow, with perched boulders on the skyline. The younger plantations give way to taller sitka spruce and lodgepole pine and the route becomes enclosed between the trees, with the noise of the rushing Dee on the right for company.

This part of the route has restricted views and there is little wildlife evident. Pylons carrying 132,000 volts of electricity stride down an unplanted strip, carrying the National Grid through Galloway. The white farm of Mid Garrary peers down the gap. Soon the bold granite peak of Cairnsmore of Dee (the Black Craig) appears ahead of the road and the Y-shaped Clatteringshaws Reservoir opens out on the right. The concrete dam is at the far end and was built in the early 1930s as part of the Galloway hydro-electric scheme. A large boulder on the east side of the loch is another Bruce's stone and commemorates another of King Robert I's victories of 1307 over the English. It is in the care of the National Trust for Scotland and is easily visited from the A712 New Galloway to Newton Stewart road.

The old Edinburgh road from Portpatrick comes through the hills to the dam to join the A712 and in the same area is the Galloway Deer Museum established by the Forestry Commission. As well as explaining the life of the red and roe deer and other fauna, the exhibition sets out to interpret the changing aspects of the Galloway landscape from the Ice Age to the present day. The Museum is open from Easter to the end of October.

Beyond the reservoir rises the granite range of Cairnsmore of Fleet and the landscape which inspired John Buchan to write his classic spy thriller *The Thirty-Nine Steps*. On this side of the Cairnsmore, the A712 passes the birthplace of Alexander Murray and the tall granite obelisk set up to his memory, but they are out of sight from the Way. Murray (1775–1813) was the son of a shepherd and has become an example, along with Burns and Carnegie, of how hard work can overcome lack of advantage and a humble background. In his 37½ years of life, Murray became one of the greatest linguists in the world and was appointed Professor of Oriental Languages at Edinburgh University.

The Way and forest road turn north, away from the distractions of Clatteringshaws, to find a route over the hills to the Glenkens. The road leads out of the forest to a locked gate and stile near a T-junction. The left branch is followed toward Mid Garrary. After several hundred metres and just before a dyke, leave the road for a track on the right, leading northwards through pastures and then north-west up a wide firebreak in the young forest. The dyke continues on the left as a guide. Turn with it to the north-east until a gap leads on a northerly course to the shallow ditched valley of the Hog Park Strand. Curleywee and Millfore are prominent hills of character to the south-west, with the big whaleback of Lamachan Hill to their right.

Firebreak and Southern Upland Way now turn towards Meikle Millyea, winding down and across the slight valley to a massive boulder and lesser satellites inside a stone dyke. A wooden hut is tethered against the storms inside the wall. The Way passes right of this feature, then leaves the firebreak to head north-east past a sheep stell and contour across the drier, grassy south-east flank of Shield Rig (320m) to reach ridge-level at its far end. The view stretches far back to Cairnsmore of Fleet, Criffel and the Lake District hills, and forward to Cairnsmore of Carsphairn, Queensberry and the Lowthers. Cairnsmore of Carsphairn is a significant landmark for the next section of the walk – but it will be a long trek yet before Queensberry is left behind. The immediate surrounds include an unusual array of glacial hummocks on Drumbuie Hill, and the high Rhins of Kells to the west.

The Galloway hills are behind and it is downhill now, through sheep country to join, just west of Clenrie, the rough road coming out of the corrie in Meikle Millyea. The house is passed on the left and the improving road followed over the Black Burn and eastward down the Garroch Glen, with forests belonging to Forrest Estate on the left. The estate is owned by Mr Fred Olsen, the Norwegian shipping magnate. Visitors to the main part of the estate in the Polharrow Glen to the north are often surprised to find Norwegian names displayed on signs and a Black Watch kilted highlander figurehead from one of his ships. The Garroch Glen has some surprises also, including the pleasant admonition: 'Fire is a constant danger in forest plantations. Please do not endanger that which we are privileged to enjoy.' Soon after this we pass the 'Thomas Olsen Road' disappearing into the forest.

The road down the glen gains a good surface opposite Drumbuie and continues past Largmore and through Knocksheen. Wildlife is abundant in this attractive glen, which has a good mix of sheep, cattle, trees both natural and planted, and man. Nature flourishes when man shows restraint. One of the most conspicuous birds to look for here is the jay, which leaves the shelter of the woodlands to feed and then flights back into the trees at hint of danger. It is a medium-sized bird with a noticeable white rump on its brown back, and blue, white and black markings on the wings.

Cattle at Knocksheen in the Garroch Glen

Beyond Over Barskeoch, the road enters Hannaston Wood where tall alders with sombre grey barks are spaced widely enough to allow an abundant spring and summer flora to develop. Carpets of bluebells and primroses with violets and herb robert add splashes of colour to the white of wood sorrel and greater stitchwort. After the road crosses the Garroch Bridge, look out for the sign pointing the route off to the left about 250m from the bridge. This leads down to a bridge back across the Garroch Burn. Turn right on the far bank once over the dyke and go along the edge of the field until a stile leads to the open hill. Slant up Waterside Hill between a birchwood (left) and a coniferous wood (right). Glenlee power station and the pipes bringing water down the hill to the turbines from Clatteringshaws Reservoir are seen to the south, past a white house.

With height gained, Corserine and the Rhins of Kells appear behind. The distinct pimple of Carlin's Cairn assumes massive dimensions when you are 13km closer to it. It is associated with Robert the Bruce at the time the outlawed king was struggling for survival among these hills. According to legend, a miller's wife from the Polmaddy Glen sheltered the outlaw and saved him from his enemies. Bruce later rewarded her with a grant of land in the glen and she, in gratitude, had her friends construct this mighty cairn on the ridge in honour of her sovereign. Sceptics may doubt the story but the cairn seems too high and remote to be a normal tumulus and must have been built for some reason.

The route follows a land-rover track over the southern face of Waterside Hill, staying above the dyke from the plantation. As the ridge is crossed, a beautiful view opens out of the Ken Valley, with the required footbridge crossing the river to Dalry. A double set of electricity transmission lines is passed. One comes up the hill from the Earlstoun power station and the other carries the National Grid. Earlstoun Loch and its dam are seen up the valley to the left, with a fish ladder leading from the reservoir to pass the near side of the power station and accompany the Way down the hill, separated by a high wire fence.

The Gordons of Earlstoun Castle were another family persecuted for their Covenanting beliefs. They were fined, banished, imprisoned, or executed, but Alexander Gordon – 'the Bull of Earlston' – is reputed to have tossed the soldiers from him when they attempted to put him to the 'boot' – a hideous piece of footwear into which wooden wedges were driven to torture the wearer.

The Way passes out of a lane to the A762 New Galloway to Carsphairn road at a cottage called Staffa, while the fish ladder turns back to the reinforced concrete power station which carries a 1936 datestone.

The Galloway Water Power Act of 1929 set in motion an ingenious hydro-electric scheme involving five power stations and seven reservoirs, plus dams, aqueducts and pipelines. On the northern side of the Southern Uplands watershed, the water from Loch Doon flowed north-westwards to the sea at the Firth of Clyde. Two dams were built to constrain the waters of the loch and a tunnel bored through the hills to the east to divert some of the reservoir's water to the south. This water, augmenting the Carsphairn Lane, joins the Water of Deugh and flows into the dammed Kendoon Loch. From there it goes down to the turbines to drive the generators before being released to flow down the Water of Ken. Next it is trapped at Carsfad Loch to generate more electricity, then released to Earlstoun Loch where it is used again.

Meanwhile the impounded waters at Clatteringshaws Reservoir are flowing down through 6km (3½ miles) of tunnel to Glenlee power station to generate power there. South of Dalry, the waters from Glenlee and Earlstoun unite and flow down Loch Ken and the River Dee, to be used yet again at Tongland power station before finally escaping to the sea at Kirkcudbright.

The Southern Upland Way turns right where it joins the A762 south of Earlstoun power station and follows the road for about 600m before turning east across the fields to the new suspension bridge over the Water of Ken, specially built for the Way by the army. St John's Town of Dalry was one of the pilgrim routes from the Central Lowlands to St Ninian's Shrine at Whithorn. James IV passed this way in 1501, using the ferry to cross the river.

On the far bank, the route joins a lane leading into the centre of Dalry, passing the ancient mote and the unusually spired town hall, to the 1917 fountain. It is worth climbing the mote for the view. A mote is an artificial mound built as a place of security. Early ones had timber stockades built round the hill-top and contained timber buildings which were easily set on fire by attackers. Larger and later motes held stone keeps. Little, however, is known about the Dalry mote.

Looking along the river-banks from the footbridge or the mote, notice the levees constructed to prevent the river from overflowing and flooding the plain. As you look into the river, consider also that some of that water may be from Loch Doon and wonder at the ingenuity of man, who has learned to coax water to flow from one side of the Southern Uplands to the other.

St John's Town of Dalry

The Ken—Nith Watershed

ST JOHN'S TOWN OF DALRY—SANQUHAR

DISTANCE: 43km (27 miles) HEIGHT RANGE: 70–580m

Only an extremely fit and experienced walker should attempt this stretch of the walk in a day. The walking is fairly straightforward in good weather, but it is a long and exposed section and can be very demanding if the weather deteriorates. It would be better to take two days for this stretch. The first part of the walk is at a relatively low level and never far from a road. However, as the walk progresses, the terrain gets higher and rougher and the roads more distant, just when a walker may be growing tired and dispirited. The problems are compounded if mist reduces visibility, making navigation difficult, or if a walker becomes 'trapped' half-way, with high ground in front and behind – as there are lots of ups and downs in this section.

Anyone committed to going north beyond Stroanfreggan can miss out part of the hill-walk by taking the public road up the Water of Ken and following the gap from Lorg to Polskeoch but this still leave an area of high ground ahead. The valleys of the Ken in the west, the Euchan Water to the north, and the Scaur, Shinnel and Dalwhat Waters to the south-east, provide possible escape routes from the Way, but it is vitally important that walkers consider well the implications of using any of them as they all involve a long walk. Everyone attempting this crossing should allow adequate safeguards against exhaustion and bad weather.

Public transport is only available at the start and finish of this section, unless escape is taken to the A713 Dalry-Carsphairn road near Polmaddie by crossing the bridges on the Water of Ken at the south end of the island of Dundeugh Hill, or by the bridge over Kendoon Loch to Carminnow. Moniaive and Tynron have a six-day bus service to Thornhill and Dumfries. This route is well off the Way but might be a life-saver if bad weather forced walkers off the ridges. The

Ayr-Castle Douglas bus service on the A713 does not operate on Sundays. The Cumnock-Dumfries service on the A76 operates seven days a week while the railway station at Kirkconnel 5km (3 miles) from Sanquhar has virtually a six-day service.

Apart from the youth hostel at Kendoon there is very little accommodation available on this, the longest section of the Way. Up-to-date information should be sought from the accommodation list produced by the Countryside Commission for Scotland, or enquire at local tourist information centres. It is essential to plan ahead. Bed-and-breakfast accommodation may be available at some places on the B729 Carsphairn-Moniaive road.

Cars can be used to break up this long walk into more manageable parts, with access from the Lochinvar road, at Butterhole Bridge, Stroanfreggan, and from the valley of the Scaur Water. Much of the route is unenclosed, with fairly rough walking, but there are some stretches of tarred road, forest road and farm tracks.

Dalry is a very pleasant and peaceful little town, yet in 1666 it was seething with discontent. Springing from the Union of the Crowns under James VI and I, various English and Episcopal traits had been introduced into the Scottish Presbyterian style of worship. The pressure for change continued during the reign of Charles I, leading to the defiant signing by thousands in 1638 of the National Covenant, pledging opposition to these innovations. This led to the Bishops' Wars and, after Charles had quarrelled with Parliament, the Civil War in an astonishing period of bargaining and counter-bargaining between the Scots, the Parliamentarians and the Royalists.

Charles I was defeated and executed, the Scots army destroyed by the Protectorate of Cromwell, and Charles II went into exile. At the restoration of Charles II in 1660, the Scots Presbyterians lost their congregational rights to appoint their own ministers and found themselves under the bishops again. In the south-west especially, many ministers left their kirks rather than consent to the bishops, and open-air services were conducted while the new ministers preached to empty churches. The Government responded by sending garrisons of dragoons into the troubled areas and fining those who attended the open-air conventicles. As bitterness increased between the two sides, violence broke out. From this time comes the legend of Grierson of Lag stabling his troopers' horses in Dalry Church and other such indignities, until the discontent in Dalry erupted into an uprising and a march on Edinburgh. This led to bloody defeat at Rullion Green in the Pentlands and a reign of terror as Covenanters were hunted down.

How are we to separate fact from propaganda three centuries later, when today's media can be so conflicting and inaccurate over issues only a few hours old? Each must draw their own conclusions from the martyrs' graves in Dalry cemetery and Glen Trool, the monument above Wigtown, Alex Linn's tomb, and other sites yet to be passed on the Way. In such a bitter conflict, no holds were barred and no opportunity missed to blacken an opponent's character. Undoubtedly there were faults on both sides and a fiendish undercurrent of intolerance existed, exemplified by the burning at the stake in Kirkcudbright of Elspeth McEwan who had been brought before the Dalry Kirk Session on charges of witchcraft in 1698 – after the re-establishment of the Presbyterian faith!

Doctrinal schisms and prejudices seem very remote and ridiculous in the peaceful Dalry of today. The Way climbs up the Main Street from the fountain, past single and two-storey terraces stepping up the hill, and the post office with its unusual old wall letter-box. Near the top of the village, the B7000 leads left on a narrow but scenic route to Carsphairn and Moniaive. Let it go and continue up the Main Street past a Victorian letter-box to a Y-junction where a worn, chair-shaped stone sits at the meeting point of the two roads.

The stone is called St John the Baptist's chair, although it is highly unlikely that John the Baptist ever visited Galloway or sat on this seat, wherever it originated. Joseph Train, the antiquarian, was mobbed in the act of trying to remove this stone for Sir Walter Scott's collection. The name St John's Town of Dalry is said to be derived from a dedication given by the Knights Templars to the local church. The order of Knights Templars was founded in 1118 to protect the right of passage for pilgrims to the Holy Land. It was first established in Scotland at Temple in Midlothian during the reign of David I.

The right fork at the junction is the direct road to Moniaive. The Way follows the left fork, passing right of Townhead Crescent and narrowing to a rough track between number 18 and Corran. The route is now bounded on either side by excellent examples of the dyker's art. Dry-stone dykes are prominent features of the Galloway landscape as Nature left an abundance of building material at hand when the glaciers melted. The examples here are superbly fitted together like jig-saw puzzles, with many small stones locking the lower courses into sturdy and shapely barriers, while the up-ended large top-stones allow the sky to show through, giving a false impression of instability to deter animals from jumping over.

We are now on the Old Edinburgh road and pass the white house of Craighead, with two rustic porches to the front and a heraldic stone on the south-west crow-stepped gable which shows three leaping animals and the initials 'W C'. Three dormer windows interrupt the roof-line to the front, each pediment having three stars and a crescent.

The track is now grassy and passes left of the big house and secluded garden of Creaganfois. In the dip just beyond it sits a curious little building of brick, corrugated sheets and ogee windows, which was once a lady's workroom. The Way now leads up to the right of a plantation alongside the dyke, to sheep country where the views open out across the knobby, outcropped foreground. There is a small reservoir in this area and extra care should be taken against pollution. Continue on the south-east side of the dyke until a stile in a corner of the field leads over to the north-west side. From the top of the steps the lochan to the west can be glimpsed, while ahead across a dip sits Ardoch Farm at the south-east corner of Ardoch Hill, with the gaunt grey stone shell of Gordonstoon on the right and black Galloway cattle scattered about the landscape.

The route leaves the dyke and heads directly across the dip, crossing another dyke by throughstones which project in steps from it. Having climbed up from the dip, the route passes west of the farm between a dyke and a copse of trees sloping down to a round lochan. A stile leads to a road and the north-west side of Ardoch. The road climbs uphill, across the south-west slopes of Ardoch Hill, but the Way leaves at right angles by a track heading between two dykes to skirt the south-eastern slopes of the hill on the edge of the wooded valley of the Trolane Burn.

Pass through a gap in a dyke running left uphill towards a cairn, and leave the valley and take a mid-course across the shoulder of the hill until the great bulks of Cairnsmore of Carsphairn and Moorbrock Hill come into view beyond Barlaes.

The scenery has changed once again, from improved farmlands to the rough grazings of the surrounding uplands. Trees are scarce now and wide sweeping skyscapes and distant ridges bring home the vastness of this countryside.

Barlaes is our pointer until the route crosses a dyke, then a tributary of the Earlstoun Burn, and turns eastwards about 600m from the farm. Mounds of stones scattered about tell again of the farmer's toil to clear the fields of glacial rubble. Perhaps early man gathered some of them together for ritual burials before early farmers cleared them from their hand ploughs. Perhaps they were built into dykes, then levelled and scattered again or built into humble dwellings which fell into ruin through time. Whatever purposes they served once, they are haphazard mounds now, settling with their secrets into the vegetation.

The Earlstoun burn is crossed by a new footbridge and the north bank followed upstream. Leave the burn and follow the far side of a dyke running uphill to the left for wide views backwards to the dark-pointed tree-clad Bennan Hill above Loch Ken, the smoother-topped Cairn Edward (named after King Robert I's brother who won a victory near New Galloway in the Wars for Independence), the high and impressive Black Craig of Dee, the smaller but abruptly faced Benniguinea farther right and the great bulky ridge of Cairnsmore of Fleet in the background over-topping all. These hills are off the route map for the Way. To the front, Cairnsmore of Carsphairn grows mightier every minute as the walker strides northwards and reminds us of the old rhyme:

'There's Cairnsmore of Fleet
And Cairnsmore of Dee
But Cairnsmore of Carsphairn's
The highest of the three.'

Indeterminate hills rolls away to the east but we have a grandstand view in this direction of the black road to Lochinvar. A dog-leg bend in the road crosses a burn by a stone bridge where three pine trees face the ruins of an old school, evidence that this empty landscape must have nurtured families in the not too-distant past.

Beyond the school ruins the road cuts through a gap and disappears round a corner to Lochinvar. From the Way we see only the small plantation at the north end of the loch and nothing of the island or site of the castle of the Gordons, from which came Sir Walter Scott's bold hero in *Marmion* to steal away a bride from her wedding ceremony. Generations of Scots schoolchildren once learned by heart:

'O, young Lochinvar is come out of the west,
Through all the wide border his steed was the best;
And, save his good broadsword, he weapons had none
He rode all unarmed and he rode all alone
So faithful in love and so dauntless in war
There never was knight like the young Lochinvar . . .'

A clandestine version circulated in the playground, where pupils weighed up the glory against the certain punishment of reciting in class:

> 'O, young Lochinvar is come out of the west
> I'll have to sit down for I don't know the rest!'

The road running west from Lochinvar meets the Moniaive road at a Y-junction. The Way, having followed the high ground west of the Lochinvar road, passes between East Barlaes Hill and the hillock to its east and descends to the road junction. The Way follows the Moniaive road now for 1½km (1 mile), uphill and down, with heather growing on either side of the road and the gobbling complaint of the red grouse generally the only sound, save the walker's footsteps.

At the Butterhole Bridge, the unfenced minor road displays a burst of ambition and takes for itself a pavement on both sides at the bridge, which carries a 1962 date for reconstruction work. A waymarked spur route on the left follows the north bank of the Black Water downstream for 3km (1½ miles) to Kendoon Youth Hostel.

The Way itself follows the road north-eastwards from the bridge for about ½km, passing a track going left to Marskaig. As the road rounds a bend it passes four trees. These are grouped around a pleasant spot west of the burn once used for a steading. The path is taken to the left here, slanting steeply up through the trees until the slope flattens out on grassy moorland. The valley is soon lost behind and the route goes north to the left of a walled green field, looking rather incongruous in its improved state in a moorland setting. Continue north, converging on another dyke. Cross this and head towards the highest point on the skyline – a rounded bump, steepest to the left. Pass round this on the left and gain the true top of Culmark Hill.

Although only 290m high, it stands well back from the high hills to the north and offers a superb view over Culmark Farm, the drumlins of the valley, and the Carsphairn-Moniaive road. Cairnsmore of Carsphairn and Moorbrock Hill look very grand and shapely to the left of the U-shaped cleft of the Water of Ken. Beyond them stretch the high ridges concealing Glen Afton. To the right of the Ken the hills are lower and less well-defined but this is the direction the Way takes and walkers should study it carefully. On Culmark Hill the Way is following the line of an old drove road which followed the Ken Valley through to Nithsdale.

Descend to Culmark Farm to the left of sheep pens, climbing over a stile and going right to the rough track. This passes left of the farm house and continues as a farm road to

Cairnsmore of Carsphairn and Moorbrock Hill from Culmark

the public highway, giving a good view west to the Rhins of Kells from the bridge over the Stroanfreggan Burn. Two ancient monuments are passed between the burn and the highway. Left of the farm road is the Stroanfreggan mote – a green mound, like an upside-down saucer. Across the farm road from it is Stroanfreggan Cairn. This was originally a large circular pile of stones built over a burial cist. When this cist was opened a skilfully made flint knife was found inside. The cairn has been robbed of many of its stones at some time in the past, probably as a convenient quarry for building dykes, and now exists in a crescentic shape.

Another ancient monument is prominent in this locality. Standing north of the highway on a rocky spine of ridge, east of the Water of Ken and guarding the entrance to that valley, is a hill-fort on Stroanfreggan Craig. The fort has been constructed on a promontory of the ridge and the natural ups and downs of the ridge were built up or excavated to render

Benbrack to Cairnsmore of Carsphairn

attack more difficult. A large, well-built cairn is conspicuous here. The rocky nature of this ridge is probably due to its exposed position at the corner of two valleys. Ancient glaciers sweeping round this corner would scalp the hillside open and grind over the slopes until all that remained was this rocky arete.

Having reached the B729 Carsphairn-Moniaive road, walkers have almost their last chance to escape to the west. Those going on with reserves of stamina, and weather and daylight in their favour, go east towards Moniaive for a short distance then turn left up the Stroanpatrick access road to a gate. Leave the road and cross the fence here and follow the outside edge of the boundary dyke of the farm, heading east. Continue for over a kilometre, staying on the north side of the dyke but avoiding the temptation to head north to the higher ground. Pass well below a plantation and at length a stile at the junction of two dykes leads on to the higher ground. The dykes are left behind and the ridges ascended to Stellhead and Manquhill Hill.

Cairnsmore of Carsphairn and its satellites, Beninner and

Moorbrock Hill, are massive to the north-west but the view to the north-east is restricted, save for the hills east of the Way. To the right of the Cairnsmore group the forested glen of the Water of Ken is attractive, with Windy Standard, Alhang, Alwhat and other high points of the ridge showing.

The Way now descends 60m as it heads for Benbrack to the north-east, passing left of a rocky boss jutting from the rather featureless moor. Cross a fence-stile in the hollow of Craigencarse and take to the Shoulder of Corlae and so on to Benbrack. This section of the walk may need skill in navigation in mist as there are few features in the landscape other than the Way-marker posts. Anyone going astray should bear south or west to the lower ground to escape back to the road. The spruce forest stretches high up the Shoulder of Corlae, and its boundary fence leads north of east to the summit of Benbrack and the Ordnance Survey trig point. This is the highest ground on the Way, apart from Lowther Hill and several points on its south-east ridge.

The view from Benbrack is excellent, embracing Hart Fell, Queensberry, the Lake District, Criffel, and the Carsphairn and Glen Afton hills. The long-distance walker can derive satisfaction from the distance covered from the Rhins of Kells, which have slipped well into the background now.

'The windy Stannart, Cairnsmore's brow,
And Moorbrock summits view we now
And to conclusion bring oor strain
On scenes we ne'er may see again.'

So wrote Thomas Murray the herd at Moorbrock in *Frae the Heather*, a volume of poems and songs which made several editions at the start of this century. Murray's hirsel at Craignell was passed at Clatteringshaws on the walk from Bargrennan to Dalry. From Craignell, Murray moved to Moorbrock, which we can see high on the moors under Cairnsmore of Carsphairn. In one of his poems, *A Dreich Trip On Duty*, Murray re-tells a marathon journey made by a herdsman of Furmiston (south of the Cairnsmore) to recover three strayed tups. Calling at Marbrack Hill, Smeaton and Stroanfreggan, the herd picked up the trail on Corlae and traversed the glens of the Appin, Shinnel, Chanlock and Scaur to Nithsdale before recovering his animals above Mennock and driving them back by Polgown, Dalgonar, Polskeoch and Lorg to Craigengillan on the Ken Water. Walkers will grow to appreciate this achievement as they pass these names on the map.

The view north from Benbrack is empty of civilisation, save for the march fence striding along the ridge and the coniferous forests girding the lower slopes. Distant elevations and encircling ridges give warning of the hard times ahead.

From here, the route follows the east side of the march fence in a north-westerly direction, then northwards along the northern ridge of Benbrack, avoiding the lower fences on either side. Stay on the east side of the main fence as it drops to a col and climb towards Coranbae Hill west of Black Hill. About half way up the slope the fence is left and an old track taken slanting to the right to the col west of Black Hill. The fence meanwhile has followed a dog-leg course over Coranbae Hill and is now regained as it climbs to Black Hill in a north-easterly direction.

As the slope eases off, the fence and the Way turn northwards a little to the north of the highest point on Black Hill. Another fence running to Colt Hill is crossed and the northern fence followed on the eastern side for High Countam. We are just within the forest area now and come to a T-junction in the fence. Follow the north-east fence (still on its east side) with forest on both sides now, and join a forest road. This leads to another road running across the Way. Cross this and maintain your course along a firebreak, following a direction sign to the nearby Allan's Cairn.

This is a square white pillar on a broader base, enclosed by a circular iron railing. Every face of the pillar is inscribed voluminously, including the pyramid capping. The main message reads:

'In memory of George Allan and Margaret Gracie
Who Followed Christ to Martyrdom
They were shot by the Dragoons of Coupland and Lagg
Near the fawns of Altry in the days of the Covenant.'

The monument was erected in 1857 and features melodramatic poetry typical of that period. It sits at a crossing of firebreaks, and the Way continues by the break to the north-west, heading towards the hills of Glen Afton, and in particular the steep spur of Polskeoch Rig hanging above the watershed of the Ken Valley. If in doubt, remember that the forest road is running in the same direction on your left. Another firebreak is crossed and the second one reached is taken to the left as the route ahead becomes blocked by forest. This new direction leads south-west to join the road, which is now followed downhill to Polskeoch. Those going in the opposite direction will see the road up to Allan's Cairn clearly from Polskeoch. If they miss the first turn-off to the cairn they can walk out to the memorial and back by the second turn-off – and then keep going south-west to High Countam.

Polskeoch sits at 360m on the watershed between the Ken/

Dee and Scaur/Nith river systems. As you approach it from Allan's Cairn the forest road sweeps round in a curve on the west side. Resist the temptation to take a short cut, which would be wet and difficult. The road-route crosses the Polvaddoch Burn twice in its curve. The forest and the Stewartry district are left east of the burn and Nithsdale entered and the tarred road joined at Polskeoch.

Electric power cables and electric fences bring the trappings of civilisation to the area, but civilisation will seem a long way away to anyone caught in a downpour in this remote spot. Such fences are charged with only a small amount of electricity to provide a mild shock to animals and deter them from rubbing against them and loosening the posts.

The road is followed now for about 4km (2¼ miles), passing a shepherd's house at Dalgonar with its sheep fanks and the upright timber posts and bar, rather like a guillotine frame, which is a standard item on a sheep farm. The frame is used for hanging the bags to be filled with the clipped wool.

At Polgown the Way leaves the road on the east side of the burn and turns left towards the farm and almost immediately turns away again to the east, round a dyke climbing uphill on the old drove road to Sanquhar and gaining height quickly as the public road twists away to the south through the glacial valley. The Polskeoch Burn has now become the Scaur Water on the right, following the U-shaped valley cut by former glaciers.

Twice crossing an electric fence by stile, we continue to slant uphill on the south-facing slopes of the ridge bounding the Scaur Valley. The road below crosses the Scaur by a metal bridge and climbs out of trouble as the burn heads for a constricted corner of the glen where it cuts its way down to a lower level in a writhing course between interlinked spurs.

Soaring above its glen rises the gully-riven precipices of Glenwhargen Craig – an unexpected sight in the midst of the rolling hills of this region. Balancing this fine view, the glen opens out to the right to show the distant Criffel and Lake District ranges.

As the Way climbs north-eastwards to Cloud Hill, Cairnsmore of Carsphairn and the Galloway hills rise behind us once again in the south-west, with the V-cut beyond Polskeoch prominent at the head of the valley of the Ken Water. The drove road to Sanquhar can become confusing in mist as it climbs from the Scaur to cross over to the Euchan Water to the north. Impatience to cross the ridge has to be resisted, as the Way stays on the southern slopes and south of a dyke until Cloud Hill is passed. The ridge becomes craggy and narrower beyond this hill and, after two small dips, a stile

Glenwhargen Craig and interlinked spurs on the Scaur Water

at last leads over the dyke to the north and a slanting course is taken north-eastwards across the northern shoulder of Welltrees Tappin about 1km (½ mile) north-west of its summit. This course crosses a fence on the shoulder at the summit of the path and with a branch of the fence on the left, continue north-eastwards, dropping down a long, gradual slope to Nithsdale.

The Lowthers now dominate the horizon on the other side of the valley, with the radar station looking rather bizarre on Lowther Hill where the Way soon has to go. The starkly cut canyons of the Mennock and Dalveen Passes slice into the curves of the high rounded slopes, and deep clefts and gullies fret the hillsides where torrents have run off after storms.

The large dark-green Ulzieside spruce plantation is a guide, as the Way passes right of it across a ditch known as the Standard Gutter. This is part of the De'il's Dyke again – which we first met on Ochiltree Hill. Here it departs in west and south-easterly directions, running across the upper slopes of the Nith Valley and keeping its mysterious purpose a secret still.

Coal measures lie directly upon the denuded edges of the Silurian strata and the Upper Nithsdale coalfield has left its mark on the landscape of the valley. Smoke-drift to the north-west reveals the small mining town of Kirkconnel where open-cast mining has temporarily ripped the green cover off the landscape on the south-west side of the town. North of the Nith stand the bings from underground workings – but all the pits are closed now. For the benefit of non-Scottish walkers, 'bing' is our delightful word for less-than-delightful waste heaps! A tall viaduct over the Crawick Water carries the railway from Glasgow to Dumfries and Carlisle.

The Way continues down the ridge west of the Whing Burn – where the carboniferous rocks are exposed – then crosses the burn just above where it joins with another burn from its east, and levels out to pass above a cottage. Three stiles in quick succession lead over dykes and a fence to join a farm track to Ulzieside. Going in the opposite direction, bear right once over the stiles and avoid a track going left, then head for the left of Ulzieside Plantation.

Those dropping to the Nith Valley and Sanquhar go round Ulzieside Farm on the left and join the public road. Go left to the bridge over the Euchan which has an 1819 datestone. Carry on to the crossroads and turn right over the River Nith at Blackaddie Bridge – a three-arch bridge with cutwaters – dated 1855. Leave the road here and follow the track along the north bank of the river south-eastwards.

The path climbs up on to a terrace between the river and the old dairy and goes round the south side of a housing scheme to Sanquhar Castle. The castle was probably built by the Crichtons in the 14th century, though some of the ruins visible are from later dates. The Way approaches the castle from the west where two sides are guarded by a steep bank. The north side is ditched. The castle consists of an outer courtyard on the west and an inner courtyard round which are grouped various buildings. The Keep in the south-east corner is the most intact of the ruins and stands beside the bakery and kitchen. The entrance gateway to the inner courtyard contains some splendid stonework but little remains of the great round tower which protected it. In the 17th century the castle was bought by Sir William Douglas of Drumlanriig, the first Duke of Queensberry. Sir William was responsible for building the magnificent castle at Drumlanrig, 14km (9 miles) to the south-east, but only stayed one night in it, preferring the humbler Sanquhar Castle. On his death the castle at Sanquhar was abandoned for Drumlanrig.

The Way leaves the ruined castle for the nearby A76 and follows it into Sanquhar, along Castle Street past an 1842 church with a wall to the side carrying the 'top of Sanquhar Cross 1680' flanked by two urns. As the main road turns into the straight, running through the town centre, the Way turns right into Leven Road for the next stage of the journey.

The entrance gate to Sanquhar Castle

The Western Lowthers
SANQUHAR—WANLOCKHEAD

DISTANCE: 13km (8 miles) HEIGHT RANGE: 140–480m

A short section – easily accomplished inside a day – leaving time to see the other attractions at each end of the route. The main problem to guard against is being caught by bad weather at Cogshead, where there is high ground to be crossed in both directions to safety. The walk passes through sheep and cattle grazing areas and an important grouse moor. J. & J. Leith Ltd. of Sanquhar run a daily bus service to Wanlockhead (Mon.-Sat.). Accommodation is very limited at Wanlockhead, save for a youth hostel, but nearby Leadhills has facilities.

Sanquhar is a thriving little town which allows the walker to rest, do some repairs, or make some purchases before tackling the Lowthers ahead. It has a 1735 Tolbooth attributed to William Adam – and also has the oldest post office in the United Kingdom. The former blocks half of the High Street, slowing the through traffic considerably. The post office, in the same street, has a projecting bow window and dates from 1763 when a Post Boy service operated on horseback, to and from Edinburgh. If you wish, you can purchase commemorative postcards here. The town holds an annual Riding of the Marches ceremony in the summer. Riding the Marches is almost exclusively a custom of the Borders Region so here is a hint that the Way is progressing and passing through a transition stage which will leave the west far behind.

Sanquhar is the gathering point for the waters of the River Nith as it cuts its way south-east through the Southern Uplands by a narrow winding valley to emerge on the plain north-west of Dumfries. The Nith divides the Uplands in two, or at least it has been superimposed on an ancient river

system to the same effect. The Nith rises on the northern slopes of the Southern Uplands near Dalmellington, and starts off by flowing north-west towards the Firth of Clyde. Then it turns north-eastwards and swings round to meander back into the Uplands on a journey to the Solway four times as long as it had to the Clyde.

North-west of Sanquhar the river valley is wide and open, save at the regional boundary under Corsencon. Between Kirkconnel and Sanquhar, the Kello, Euchan and Crawick waters augment the Nith, and road, railway and river squash together beyond Mennock to win a way to the south. In the case of the river it is probable that the Nith at one time did flow to the Clyde but by glacial breaching to the south-east and damming up to the north, the Nith was diverted into another valley.

Sanquhar is certainly a very significant juncture on the Southern Upland Way. Crossing the Nith brings a welcome sense of achievement. The road, railway and commercial life of this small industrial and agricultural town offers a variation from the wide-sweeping uplands. Ahead lies a totally new type of scenery with the thin shales of the Lowthers crumbling away to produce smooth curving green slopes. The names Nithsdale, and Clydesdale and Annandale beyond the Lowthers, denote social and cultural changes as well. Other names, like cleuchs and linns, appear on the map to join or replace the fells, craigs, rigs, knowes, knocks, burns, flows and mosses of Galloway.

At the south end of Sanquhar's High Street stands a tall obelisk on the site of the town cross, where in 1680 Richard Cameron fixed a declaration renouncing allegiance to Charles II. Cameron was killed by dragoons near Cumnock in the same year. This Sanquhar Declaration was followed in 1685 by the Sanquhar Protestation which James Renwick nailed up in the same place against the usurpation of James VII. Renwick went to the scaffold three years later as one of the last Covenanter martyrs.

The Way leaves the south end of the High Street, not far from the obelisk, and turns north by Leven Road past the fire station and the bus garage of J. & J. Leith Ltd. Then under a railway bridge where an immediate right turn and left turn leads to a long straight and steady climb out of the town, up the Cow Wynd and Matthew's Folly. The view improves all the way – back to Ulzieside Plantation and the hills back to

The High Street in Sanquhar with the obelisk on the site of the town cross

Carsphairn, to Kirkconnel, Corsencon and the Nith Valley, to Eliock to the south and to Sanquhar with its castle and railway below.

Eliock House was the birthplace in 1560 of James Crichton, the youthful prodigy remembered as 'The Admirable Crichton'. With a mastery of a dozen languages and skill in swordmanship, music, dancing, poetry and other graces, Crichton liked the limelight, but paid for it with a violent death in a brawl at the age of 20, when acting as tutor to the Duke of Mantua's son.

The railway is the former Glasgow and South Western line opened in 1850 to Dumfries and Carlisle in opposition to the Caledonian Railway Company's route by Beattock. The Beattock route has won the main traffic today between Glasgow and London. However, British Rail still run services through Sanquhar, but trains have not stopped here since 1965. There is still a passenger service to nearby Kirkconnel station. One of the reasons for retaining the line is that it carries traffic from Stranraer which has had to come north through Ayr and Kilmarnock since the line by Newton Stewart and Castle Douglas to Carlisle through Galloway was a victim of the 1965 cuts. If it is not too discouraging for the walk ahead, walkers may care to consider the three hours it takes a train to come the long way round from Stranraer by Kilmarnock to Sanquhar – and compare that with their own performance on the more direct route over the hills!

The walk up the hill from the town is popular and benches are provided at intervals for the faint. A flagpole is passed near the top of the hill then the route continues along a farm road until the road bends to the right. Go straight on here along a rough lane across the table-top of Sanquhar Moor, heading through a firebreak in a small plantation towards the open hills again. The track and Way bend left to the road first, which is followed eastwards to Dinanrig. Here it splits left to Clenries and right to Bog and Brandleys. Take the right-hand road and fork left away from Bog and north of a plantation. Clenries is seen well to the left among trees, while the steep V-sided valley away to the east was a hiding place for Peden the prophet, the minister from New Luce, during the Killing Time.

Leave the road north of the plantation and take a course to the left, heading north-eastwards over the coarse grassy slopes to cross the ridge in front. Conrig Hill on the left and an unnamed equivalent height at the right-hand end are the highest points on the ridge in front. The Way crosses this ridge between these two tops by ascending the ridge to a shoulder to the left of the low nick. While this may appear to

The Lowther Hills from Bog. The valley on the left was a hiding place for 'Peden the Prophet'

be higher than necessary, it is a good line and the shortest way. An electric fence runs up the ridge just to the right of the route and solves route-finding problems in mist as it leads to the col where a non-electrified fence is crossed.

In clear weather, walkers should see to the Carsphairn hills at least, New Cumnock and Kirkconnel, and from Corsencon to Criffel down the Nith Valley.

Now the route goes over a soggy wet col to a wider track right of a little gully and a view down to the ruined house at Cogshead. The Cog Burn changes direction at the house. Flowing south-west to the house, it turns north beyond the house and makes its way deep down in the valley at a lower level to join the Crawick Water. It is almost as though Cogshead sat at the lip of a lateral hanging valley and the impression is heightened by a forest road U-bending along the valley walls, with its cross-over point just below the house. Vast denudation of the Southern Uplands has left few clues to the original pattern of their rivers but greater forces than the Cog Burn seem to have been at work here in cutting out this deep valley. The valley is afforested west of the house, while the slopes to the east are grassy and well stocked with sheep.

Horizontal and crescent-shaped drainage lines around the slopes point to extensive management work.

The Way descends to Cogshead from the col, following an old coffin route which climbs out of the valley again over Glengaber Hill to Wanlockhead. The route to Cogshead is down a turf spur joining the road just inside the forest before it crosses the burn. The derelict hip-roofed house is passed on the west, then comes a choice of routes.

The main route leaves the forest road at a stile and heads east above the house to turn the south-west spur of Lawmill Knowe, then works north round the head of a burn and climbs north-eastwards on a fairly clear path to a gate and the col west of Glengaber Hill. The path becomes a very distinct vehicle track at the col and this is easily followed down to the Wanlock Water through the heather and past grouse shooting butts.

Walkers should take care to avoid causing disturbance, especially during the April-May nesting season and during the grouse shooting season, starting on the 12th of August. The alternative route – indicated by an estate sign – is longer but is easier to follow in mist as it follows the forest road all the way. This runs northwards above the east side of the Cog Burn and cuts north-east over the north-west ridge of Lawmill Knowe to curl across the valley of the Glensalloch Burn. This valley is another deeply cut and impressive gap in the landscape and as the road makes its way round to the eastern slope, it passes the astonishing sight of the wreck of an abandoned ice cream van in a quite incongruous setting. The forested areas are comparatively small and well integrated with sheep farming here.

The valley is left south-east of Wedder Dod and as the road turns north-eastwards, Tinto Hill stands to the front beyond the farms on the Crawfordjohn to Sanquhar road. Cairn Table is prominent to the north-west at Muirkirk, with its massive summit cairns making little knobs on the horizon. The drama is going from the landscape now though, the contours spread themselves wider under the forest, and the Way takes to the right at a T-junction and wends its way eastwards with several wriggles in the road to wind round the next ridge.

As it does so, the road drops to Duntercleuch and the view opens out up the Wanlock Water to Wanlockhead and the strange ornaments on Lowther Hill. The alternative route by Duntercleuch and the main route by the Glengaber Pass meet up on the east bank of the Wanlock Water to follow a wider track south-eastwards to Wanlockhead.

The landscape has undergone astonishing change, yet

again bringing fresh variety and experience to the cross-country walker. The forests and grasslands to the west have given way in colour and texture to grouse moors about and above the Wanlock Water. The paths on both routes look down into an industrial landscape of grey spoil heaps and abandoned mine workings.

Some countryside-lovers who abhor industry and the hand of Man may find the Wanlockhead area unsightly and may close their minds to its rich heritage. To the uninitiated, the scars and waste heaps of centuries of mining may come as blots on the Southern Uplands landscape. To think so is to ignore a unique village and a fascinating stretch of the walk, rich in social history. The hill-top radar station beyond the village is only one of the latest innovations to a landscape that has been changing for centuries.

As the descent is made to the Wanlock Burn, interest focuses on an area of large grey concentric circles carved out of the detritus at the foot of Sowen Dod. This was part of a lead smelter built by the Duke of Buccleuch and Queensberry in the mid-19th century. Coal and peat were used for fuel and lime as a flux. When lead ore was added to this, a strong air blast was directed into the mixture to raise the temperature and melt the lead. The fumes were led away into long, timber-lined tunnels where the gases condensed and the valuable residue of lead and silver could be salvaged for re-smelting. Although many of the timbers have rotted away, the outlines of these remarkable fume tunnels remain etched on the hillside, a fitting prelude to the fascinating village the Way is now entering.

Wanlockhead at 425m is the highest inhabited village in Scotland. With the village of Leadhills 2km (1 mile) away, at a slightly lower altitude, it presents an enigma to the first-time visitor to explain how such substantial communities can survive and prosper in such a remote and harsh environment. Although the climate is severe and the communications difficult, by one means or another a thriving population has existed here for centuries in Tibetan-like fortitude and showing admirable enterprise.

The mineral wealth of the area attracted prospectors as far back at least as the Middle Ages. The title of the Rev. J. Moir-Porteous's book *God's Treasure House in Scotland*, written here in the 19th century, gives the clue to the wealth of natural resources being mined from the area at that time. What cannot be so easily explained is the vitality of the communities today, now that mining has ceased.

Gold was discovered in this area in the Middle Ages. Panning and re-panning of the alluvial deposits by the burns through the centuries appears to have exhausted the supply, but lead and other minerals remain in quantity and may be worked again some day, once their value exceeds the cost of extraction.

The earliest lead miners may have been the Romans, as they certainly explored the area. A mine was in operation in 1512 and by the 18th century a considerable industry had developed and the problems of driving tunnels, constructing mine shafts, furnaces and water channels were exercising the brains of some of the best engineers of the time.

Mining carried on intermittently into the 20th century for lead, zinc and other minerals but the most recent commercial extractions ceased in the 1950s. Wanlockhead is still very much alive, though, and visitors are at once struck by the spirit of expansion rather than contraction which is visible.

The Wanlockhead Museum Trust has done great work in promoting the village's attractions and thousands of visitors are drawn here each year to explore the mining trails, hunt for minerals, and learn about the area, its history, industries, and people.

The Wanlockhead Beam Engine

The smelter opposite Glengaber Hill is the first of many interesting features the Way passes on its route through Wanlockhead. The road on the north side of the Wanlock Water is followed south-eastwards to Meadowfoot which is a detached part of the village. In the old burial ground here, the memorial stones add their bit to the social history of the district, recalling miners, overseers, managers, washers, smelters, enginemen and engineering smiths back to the 18th century.

Just off the road to the east is the Waterwheel Pit and the Bay Mine, where William Symington's first commercial atmospheric pumping engine worked at the end of the 18th century. The bed for a horse tramway can be seen on the slope running from the Bay Mine back to the Smelter.

As the first houses of the village proper are reached, the Way leaves the road and goes downhill to the right, past Pates Knowes to cross the burn and climb above a cottage to follow the trackbed of an old narrow-gauge railway into the village. Pates Knowes was a lead smelt mill in 1764. The site has been excavated and partly reconstructed to show the hearths, waterwheel pit and ancillary areas. John Smeaton (rebuilder of the Eddystone Lighthouse) designed the ore crusher at this smelter.

The toxic fumes from lead smelting were a constant health problem and as civilisation slowly progressed, smelters were banished farther and farther from habitations. Pates Knowes replaced a smelter farther up the village and it in turn was replaced by the Meadowfoot Smelter. Looking over Pates Knowes from the view indicator, the steep spoil heaps of the New Glencrieff Mine are seen in the background. The mine is the one most recently worked in the area but it has a long history. In the 20th century its shaft was sunk 460m, taking it 120m below sea-level.

The Southern Upland Way now follows the Visitor Walkway from Pates Knowes along the old railway-bed, with white marker stones denoting the route. An indicator plinth looks across the Wanlock Burn to the village and offers a comparison now with the scene as it was drawn in 1775 by John Clerk of Eldin.

Then we pass the Wanlockhead Beam Engine which is now a scheduled industrial monument. Constructed from a heavy wooden beam, a wooden water bucket and iron parts, it was used to drain the Straitsteps Mine in the 19th century. The beam pivoted above a pillar of dressed freestone, with the water bucket attached to one arm and a pump piston on the other. In operation, as the bucket filled with water from a cistern on the hillside, its weight outweighed the column of

The Memorial to the poet Robert Reid, at Wanlockhead Library

water above the pump piston. The bucket fell, lifting the water on the other arm into the drainage level 27m below ground. The water in the bucket was released by a valve into a culvert leading to a burn, causing the pump rod and piston to drop again, and the bucket to rise empty to start the process all over again.

A circular horse-walk in front of the beam engine was a separate device for winding the lead ore up the shaft. A working model of the beam engine can be seen in the indoor museum farther up the Trail.

The church by the road was built in 1848. In 1861 Wanlockhead was made a 'quoad sacra' parish – that is, one established to provide additional church accommodation but without the civil functions. Prior to this a chapel existed in 1753 but, before that, the miners' families had to face the long walk over the hills to Sanquhar and back by Cogshead to attend the parish church. Funeral parties fared the same. Way-walkers would hardly regard such a Sunday as a 'day of rest' or relish the prospect of carrying a coffin there!

Between the burn and the road is the entrance to the Loch Nell Mine. This is open to visitors from 13.00 to 15.30 daily from Easter to September. Tickets are issued at the museum

The partly restored smelt-mill at Pates Knowes and the New Glencrieff Mine

nearby, which is open from 11.00 to 16.00 daily in the same season. Visitors are issued with helmets and conducted about 300m into the mine to see the ore veins, a shaft dropping to the low level, and a surprise tableau as extra lighting is switched on to reveal the tunnel ahead peopled with life-size models toiling in the conditions of by-gone days.

From the mine entrance, the route continues alongside and over the much-constrained burn to rejoin the road. Across it sits the Mining Museum at the site of the miners' forge. This is an essential stop for anyone wishing to understand the area. It houses displays on the working and living conditions of the miners, the technology of mining, geological specimens, and the history of the railway, as well as being a useful information office and sales point.

The brae to the left rises past the old manse and the former school to the Miners Library. This was founded in 1756 – 15 years after the library at Leadhills started up as the first community subscription library in Britain. A bronze tablet on the outside wall of the Wanlockhead Library commemorates the local poet, Robert Reid. Farther up the street is the youth hostel.

Wanlockhead from the slopes of Lowther Hill

The Eastern Lowthers

WANLOCKHEAD—BEATTOCK

DISTANCE: 32km (20 miles) HEIGHT RANGE: 100–710m

This lengthy section crosses both the highest point and mid-point on the Way. It is interrupted by the A702 Elvanfoot-Thornhill road and the road at Daer, and joins a road at the last part of the walk, near Beattock. It is not a difficult walk for experienced people but it can be very exacting and much depends on the weather. The high ground around Lowther Hill and beyond the Daer Reservoir is often under cloud and can be very unpleasant – and potentially dangerous – under certain conditions of wind, rain or snow. Less-experienced walkers should restrict themselves to shorter sections of the route in good weather, going out and coming back to the same point without crossing the ridges. A Dumfries to Thornhill and Edinburgh bus service operates on the A702, otherwise public transport is restricted to the ends of the section. The area is an important catchment basin for public water supplies so care should be taken against causing pollution. There are camp-sites at Beattock and Moffat and a wide range of services and accommodation in the Beattock and Moffat area. Walkers intending to do this section of the route in two stages will need to plan accommodation in advance.

Having reached the highest village in Scotland, many travel downhill now – cyclists and hikers who have toiled up to the hostel from Mennock or Elvanfoot, homing pigeons sent up for release at the highest point on the road, motorists on holiday or on business trips, crossing from one side of the country to another, and in the past, horses and carts carrying lead from the mines for shipment from the docks at Leith to Europe – until the railway took over this arduous work. However, the Way-walker's route is still upwards!

Starting from the museum at the junction of three roads,

from Meadowfoot, the youth hostel and the library, and the access road from the Mennock to Leadhills road, the Way climbs through the open space used as a car park and ascends the grassy banks to join the Beggars Brae and cross the B797 Leadhills road. Follow a Scottish Rights of Way Society sign directing you right of the new cemetery and across the trackbed of the light railway.

The line ran from Wanlockhead to Leadhills and Elvanfoot, where it linked with the Glasgow-Carlisle main line. The line's summit at 457m where it entered Wanlockhead was the highest on British standard-gauge passenger railways. It was sanctioned by a Light Railway Order of 1898 and built by Charles Foreman and Robert McAlpine & Sons, the civil engineer and construction company who were also responsible for the scenic and spectacular West Highland line. The Wanlockhead branch line from Elvanfoot was a modest 11½km (7¼ miles) long but rose 210m in a stiff pull with a maximum gradient of 1 in 40. The route was almost unfenced, so locomotives were fitted with cow-catchers and were restricted to a maximum speed of 20mph. Passengers were carried as well as minerals in short trains of mixed rolling stock. There were no platforms at Wanlockhead or Leadhills and no signals on the line. The Caledonian Railway Company opened the line to Leadhills in 1901, and to Wanlockhead in 1902. All traffic ceased in 1939.

To the west of the Way, and just below the line of the railway, is the headgear for an inclined plane. Bars of smelted lead were hauled from the Meadowfoot Smelter on the narrow-gauge railway to the foot of the incline and then winched up by compressed air to join the train in the sidings.

The complex of buildings just above the new cemetery was once a military camp. Part of it subsequently functioned as a hotel, advertising itself as the highest in Scotland. The hotel was closed – but may be re-opened – and a school has taken over some of the buildings as an outdoor centre. Go right of the end buildings and over a stile and head straight up the slope and across the south-west slope of Stake Hill. A contour is made across the head of the Mossy Burn looking over to its little reservoir, across to the Mennock Pass – down which the B797 road to Sanquhar runs under the gullies and ravines of the Lowthers. Then a southerly course is taken to join the private access road which runs to the top of Lowther Hill, leaving the Enterkin Pass public right of way to continue to the south beyond a bend in the road.

The road is flanked by red and yellow marker poles which may seem unnecessary in summer. In winter, when the road

The summit of Lowther Hill from Stake Hill

The Radar Station at the summit of Lowther Hill

often disappears under snow, they can be the only clue to the road's whereabouts for the personnel who maintain the 24 hours manning of the radar station. Steering a line between the left-hand edge of the road (yellow posts) and the right (red posts) going up, and reversing the order coming down, vehicle drivers contrive to stay on the road. The white-lining conscientiously marked up the crown of this generally traffic-free road is likewise of great benefit in mist or darkness at other times of the year.

The road is followed round an S-bend then a short-cut is taken left of the road up the north-west ridge of Lowther Hill with a fence and a turf wall (of ancient origin but later followed by county and regional boundaries) for company. The road zig-zags up across the line of the Way and into the compound of the Civil Aviation Authority's radar station, which is dominated by the two huge and impressive golf-ball-like radar containers which can be seen from far away. The station was established in 1948. Jet trails high overhead are frequent reminders of the aircraft movements over these hills and the importance of the CAA's work in regulating them.

The road and the Way part company near the summit. The

road continues along the ridge to the GPO's installations on the neighbouring Green Lowther. Wind speeds of over 100mph have been recorded on this ridge. In such conditions, no walker should be anywhere near the ridge as even the heavy iron stanchions of the GPO aerials have collapsed before the blast.

The view from Lowther Hill's slopes and summit is very extensive. Wanlockhead appears as an undisciplined but not unattractive clutter of buildings, reflecting the haphazard development of a pioneering community remote from planning legislation. A patchwork quilt of strip-burning of the heather for grouse management covers the hills above, and Cairn Table lies to the north-west. Leadhills shows to the right at its slightly lower elevation, beyond a reservoir. It is another community with a long tradition of mining. Gold from Leadhills is included in the Crown of Scotland. Allan Ramsay the poet was born in Leadhills in 1686. He, along with James Stirling, gave the village its circulating library in 1741, the first of its kind to be formed in Britain. In the cemetery at Leadhills is a remarkable gravestone to John Taylor, making him 137 when he died. An obelisk just outside the cemetery commemorates William Symington, the pioneer of steam navigation, who was born in the village.

To the right of Leadhills stands Tinto Hill and the Pentlands with the Central Lowlands beyond. Ravenscraig Steel Works and the multi-storey flats at Motherwell can be seen in moderately good weather. In clearer weather, Ben Lomond, Ben Vorlich, Stuc a' Chroin and other peaks of the Grampians rise above the smoke haze of the Lowlands. They are best seen in anti-cyclonic conditions in winter, when cold air traps the smoke in the valleys and the snow-capped peaks sparkle in the clear upper air. Snow lies on the Lowthers from time to time when the north-facing gullies trap the drifting snow and skiers take advantage of the high roads to reach the slopes, though most skiers on Lowther Hill tend to be locals. The summit of Lowther Hill was once a graveyard for suicide cases in the district, who were considered unfit to be buried in the churchyard.

The Southern Upland Way reaches its highest point on Lowther Hill (710m, just 15m below the summit) and passes round the right-hand side of the radar station fence to a stile over an electric fence to the west. Cross the fence, pass a grey square shed, contour left over the slope, and follow the fence along the tundra-like vegetation of the south ridge. The Enterkin Pass is below to the west – a steep-sided valley cut by the Enterkin Burn rising to a 540m col west of Lowther Hill before descending to Wanlockhead. At one time it was an

Looking west from the col between Lowther Hill and Cold Moss

important road through the uplands. A party of dragoons was ambushed here and its Covenanter prisoners released by their friends. Prince Charlie's Jacobite army also came this way in 1745 when retreating from Derby. Now the pass is seldom used.

Thornhill and Dumfries are visible from this shoulder of the hill in clear weather, with the Nith estuary behind and Criffel, Screel, Bengairn and Cairnsmore of Fleet to the right. Then comes the Rhins of Kells with the Merrick behind and Cairnsmore of Carsphairn to the right. On the far horizon stand the Lake District hills and it is said that Arran, Jura and Ireland can also be seen.

The Over Fingland march fence, which also marks the boundary between Strathclyde and Dumfries and Galloway, is followed down the ridge. Where the fence turns to the left, cross over to the north side and follow it east then south-east down the slope. From this turn in the fence, Tinto is visible again to the north-east, with Hartfell, Saddle Yoke and the Ettrick hills beyond the Daer Reservoir. The Devil's Beef Tub – where stolen cattle were hidden – can be identified left of Hart Fell by the prominent little rounded cone called the 'Crown of Scotland'.

The Daer Reservoir is of particular interest, not only because the Way must pass it, but also because it is now an unusual event to see a large sheet of water in the landscape. Since crossing the Nith, the vegetation has changed to short, tawny grass and moss, the slopes have become drier, the lochs have been left behind and the wildlife is changing. Blue or mountain hares are much more common on the Lowther ridges than farther west, the golden plover's sad calls rend the air, and flocks of snow buntings bustle among the grasses.

Stay with the fence as you drop to the col between Lowther Hill and Cold Moss. Then it's a steep pull up again to Cold Moss and on along the fence to Comb Head. The Dalveen Pass to the south is very impressive, with steep sweeping slopes on either side of the flat valley floor and the Toll Cottage and cars tiny on the winding road.

Above the pass, a red-roofed hut is conspicuous in front of trees sheltering the white walls of Troloss. On the other side of the road, a modern house is almost hidden under the hills, separated by a small plantation from a private cemetery – the family burial ground of the former tenants of Troloss.

The fence doubles up with an old dyke as the ridge is followed down and up to Laght Hill, where another fence and dyke join from the south, but take care to stay on the north side of the dyke at this point. Green Lowther is prominent from Laght Hill and constant traffic pinpoints the busy A74 Glasgow-Carlisle road away to the north-east beyond the Watermeetings Forest. Turn left with the fence and dyke, heading towards the north-east top of Laght Hill and cross the col to a stile. Go east down the field, south of the farm and the small plantations, and emerge on the main road at Troloss Cottage – which sits just below Over Fingland.

The road here is the A702 Carronbridge to Elvanfoot, which was seen from Comb Head climbing the Dalveen Pass. It was constructed about 1800, joining under Laght Hill a Roman Road running through the Well Pass from Durisdeer to Crawford. Turn left along the modern road and look for traces of the Roman Road as the two run north-east more or less concurrently to the Potrenick Burn, mid-way between Over Fingland and Nether Fingland.

The red surface on the road is a feature of minor Lanarkshire roads, due to the use of a red felsite from the Cairngryffe Quarry near Lanark. It is applied as a surface dressing to a Cationic Bitumen Emulsion and gives a pleasant warmth to the landscape. It is noticeable around Wanlockhead and Leadhills also, while on the road up

Over Fingland and the Potrail Water

Lowther Hill the stone was pre-coated and used in a wearing course which gave a black surface to the road. This is now wearing red in patches as the stone becomes polished by traffic.

Just after the road crosses the Potrenick Burn, the Way leaves the road on the right, goes through a gate and heads north-east towards the Potrail Water, to meet it about 100m above where the Potrenick Burns joins it.

Cross a new bridge at a water intake channel for the Peden Water Scheme farther down the valley (which supplies Cambusnethan and the higher parts of Wishaw) and turn northwards over a stile for a short distance along the Potrail Water before meeting a wide grassy ride running east towards Pin Stane. Follow this straight uphill into Watermeetings Forest to the metalled forest road running south-east. Pause here to reflect: you are at the half-way point of the Southern Upland Way! The Way now follows the forest road south-east and then south round the slopes of Pin Stane, and across the western slopes of the Pin Stane-Coom Rig col. Continue with it through the gap of the Benuff Burn between Coom Rig and

The Daer Reservoir from Sweetshaw Brae

Little Shag. The road now emerges from the forest and is followed over its summit as it swings round eastwards across open slopes, looking down the Daer Valley which inspired a book of poems *From Daer Water* by Bessie J. B. MacArthur.

The road descends again, passing north of the first two outlying blocks of forest, then entering the Hitteril Hill Plantation and descending to join the public road west of the Daer Reservoir.

The Daer Reservoir Water Scheme was opened in 1956, becoming the largest scheme in Lanarkshire. The present capacity is 5600 million gallons with a daily output of approximately 28½ million gallons. This is approximately half of the total daily demand in the Lanarkshire area. The reservoir embankment is 800m (½ mile) long and 40m above the original stream bed. At the time of its construction it was possibly one of the largest earth dams in Britain.

The public road is followed down the valley from the dam and over the bridge on the Daer Water. (Those going in the opposite direction take the second forest road after this bridge.) Where the road comes to a T-junction, the public road goes left and the service road right to the water treatment works and water workers' houses. Take neither, but go straight on up the slope between the Hapturnell Burn and a plantation to the south. Once above the trees, turn the corner south-eastwards and contour above the plantation and treatment works until a dyke leads left up Sweetshaw Brae where the Way follows over a stile.

The reservoir stretches impressively to the south-west, ringed by high hills culminating in Queensberry. Several houses now lie under the water, the occupants having been re-housed higher up the slopes. Among the numerous burns converging on the Daer, several can claim to be the source of the River Clyde. The Way looks directly along the dam and down to the treatment works, where the natural colour is removed from the raw water by chemical means. Beyond the works and houses stretches Watermeetings Forest and, high in the background, is the unique skyline of Lowther Hill and Green Lowther. Follow the dyke up Sweetshaw Brae and, as it levels out and the dam disappears, the route passes over a broad corridor of disturbed ground crossing the hillside in a south-easterly direction. This was an excavation for a gas pipeline constructed in the 1970s.

The ridge boundary has now become a fence as it runs up to the unnamed summit (567m) between Mid Hill and Hods Hill. Then it reverts to a dyke running along the regional boundary to the south-east, before rising over Hods Hill (550m) and running on south-westwards down and up as a dyke to Beld Knowe (512m). The Moffat and Ettrick hills now loom large on the horizon across Annandale. The long-distance walker, delighted that the half-way point on the Way is now past, will be pleased to know that the Ettrick hills ahead mark the start of the Borders!

From Beld Knowe, go south with the dyke still on your left hand. When the dyke turns to the south-east, go on south for 20m and join a wide grassy track running west to east across the slope. If the weather is misty stay with the dyke, which converges (as a fence) with the track at a gate and stile on the east side of the ridge. The Way is downwards to the south-east now, off the Daer catchment area and into Annandale. The Daer flows northwards to join the north and west-flowing Clyde. The Annan flows south to the Solway and the Irish Sea. Apart from the Daer and a few small streams, all the rivers encountered so far have gone south. The Annan and its tributaries are almost the last of the south-flowing streams met on the Southern Upland Way. Soon, most valleys will be leading eastwards to the North Sea.

The route down into Annandale is by the firm and stony

access track which was crossed earlier. The track enters a young forest and in one or two places is eroded badly by the run-off of burns after storms. Forests can affect the drainage pattern considerably, with ditches channelling flood water into larger streams which can scour the hillside. Once a rivulet grooves a course into the relatively soft surface of the road, its work is carried on by the next downpour. Wooden sleepers have been used to consolidate the road in places and white marker poles peg out the route across the landscape. As the track descends the south-west slopes of Shiel Hill through the plantations, two grey buildings come into view at Brattleburn – one roofed and one ruinous. The shepherd's cottage at Mosshope lies farther down the valley but the track swings right across a clearing and the Cloffin Burn before reaching it. A memorial stone passed by the Way here reads 'J Wat Died Jan 1794'.

As the track heads south and steeply uphill again across the col west of Craig Hill, the Way leaves it at a stile and goes south-east along the lower end of a plantation to pass south of Mosshope and join the forest road leading to the house. The road is followed along the forested southern slopes of the valley on the north side of Craig Hill looking across the Cloffin Burn to cattle and sheep pastures on a rocky edge of Greskine Forest.

To the east, the burn wriggles its way round glacial drumlins to join the Evan Water in the major valley. How major it is is shown over the tree-tops by the steady stream of traffic speeding between Glasgow and London. The forest road being followed climbs to a T-junction and the Way goes along the right branch towards Rivox. At the col between Craig Hill and Rivox Moor an access track reappears to make a cross-roads with the road to Rivox. Turn left downhill following the track south-eastwards between the newly planted slopes of Rivox Moor and the open pastures beside the Rivox Burn. To the right is the large grey farmhouse at Rivox, with a long white barn to the north. The hill-tops here are forested while the valley-floor is grazed by sheep – a position that is usually reversed in other areas. Cross the Rivox Burn and continue south-eastwards to the Garpol Burn. Cross the wooden bridge here which carries a plaque presented by army apprentices in memory of L/Cpl Foy V. and recording the erection of the bridge by 1 Troop, 118 Sqn RETA, September 1982. The Garpol is a very attractive glen lower down, with several ancient monuments.

From Foy's Bridge continue south-east, going uphill well to the right of the old farm of Holmshaw and following a very wide ride for about 1½km (1 mile). After a dip, a firebreak is followed slanting right. Another is taken to the right after about 300m. This curves slightly right then left again and comes to a T-junction after about 200m. Go left and emerge at an artificial pond surrounded by amenity planting. This is an attractive corner, with daffodils in spring, vivid colour in autumn, and pleasure at all seasons to attract the public off the nearby road.

This road is now followed eastwards to Beattock. Those going to Daer should leave the road for the track to the pond in the dip just after the forest and before Easter Earshaig. Then go north-west and work right on to the big ride which is running parallel.

The road from Easter Earshaig has an attractive view south-west to Queensberry, then a short section of Earshaig Forest is walked and a monument passed on the left as the road re-emerges from the trees. This is a sandstone tablet to Ben Wilson of Holmshaw 'who was killed by lightning on the 11th August 1897'.

Beld Knowe and the line of the Southern Upland Way can be seen a long way behind. To the north-east is the massive spread of Hart Fell with the undulating ridge of the Ettricks farther south. Over the brow of the hill we look towards the important native hill-top fort of Burnswark, near Lockerbie, identified by its flat-topped wedge shape, while to the south-west among the harder grits the pointed peak of Wee Queensberry shows above the ridges of Queensberry. The Romans took over Burnswark from the inhabitants, using siege tactics.

As the Way follows this elevated part of the road, in breaking out from the Lowthers it passes through an area studded with hill-forts overlooking Annandale. This valley is an important trade route today and must have been in prehistoric days as well. The Romans found it a strategic route through to Clydesdale, as their camps and forts show along the course of the road they built below. Were earlier races knowledgeable and organised enough to use the geography of the region to their advantage? Is it just coincidence that Beattock Hill Fort looks to Burnswark Fort across 26km (16½ miles) of countryside, or was it chosen by the Romans, or even tribes pre-dating the Romans, as a signalling point? We may never know, but reflecting on these matters may give us a little humility as we tramp Scotland's hills. A few modern walkers may have inflated ideas about their prowess, whilst the more perceptive may sometimes get the feeling that it has all been done before – long ago.

The ancient earthworks on Beattock Hill have been augmented by 20th-century earthworks now. The hill is a tip for the local district council, but only a corrugated shed and boundary fence give the show away to the casual passer-by, and dumped rubbish is well-screened from view by the contours of the hill. Most eyes are on the distance by now, anyway, as a glorious view is unfolded across Annandale where the road turns the corner for its steep descent. Beattock lies below to the right and Moffat behind to the left.

Running across the base of the scene is the Glasgow-Carlisle West Coast main-line railway, opened by the Caledonian Railway Company in 1848. The dignified crow-stepped gabled station at Beattock was closed to passengers in 1972 but still functions as a small maintenance depot. Frequent electric locomotive-hauled passenger trains hurtle down Beattock Bank at over 160km/hr (100mph), joining Glasgow to London in a 5¼-hour journey now, and Edinburgh to the Midlands in under 5 hours. Northbound trains take the bank easily in their stride, whereas in the 'romantic' days of steam, banking engines often had to be coupled on to trains at Beattock to assist them struggle up the slope in a long drawn-out confrontation with gravity. The Advanced Passenger Train was brought into service on this line in 1982, cutting the time from Glasgow to London to 4¼ hours. Difficulties with the tilting mechanism, which allowed the train to corner at high speeds brought about its withdrawal again. Its future is still uncertain at the time of writing.

Behind the railway, and slightly elevated above it, sits the A74 highway from Glasgow to Carlisle with the Moffat road underpassing it from Beattock. In direct competition with the railway, inter-city coaches and long-distance lorries roar up and down the road all day and night, with vans, cars and other vehicles passing and being passed in an endless chase. Some road-users criticise the A74 and dub it a 'killer road' for its reputed high accident figures. Drivers coming north from motorways in England sometimes find it difficult to adjust to the hazards of this long-distance dual carriageway – but roads don't cause accidents, drivers do. The walker, however, is provided with an underpass when the A74 is reached beyond Beattock.

The Evan Water winds across the plain but the Annan is difficult to see. There is plenty of other variety in the bounded fields, multiplicity of tree-belts, scattered farms, rural houses, and the square tower of Lochhouse dominated by the high hills cleft by the valley of the Moffat Water. Some walkers may find another busy valley distasteful, with the hand of Man evident again, even in the green fields. Life becomes very dull if we gut it of contrasts. One of the great delights of the Southern Upland Way is this range of contrasts experienced between the west and east coasts. Most walkers will relish Annandale as a diversion from the lonely moors, forests and ridges they have encountered and will quicken their step to join in the action as they stride down the Crooked Road. Even those who dislike civilisation will feel keyed-up with anticipation as they view the distant tracks winding up into the Ettricks, where the Way progresses.

As the road takes a bridge over the railway line it is a stimulating experience to watch an inter-city express hurtle through the station, powered by the overhead 25kv electric cables. Look to the north side of the bridge also for another piece of railway history – in the curved course of the more leisurely branch line which led off from here to Moffat in the days of steam between 1883–1954.

Beattock Farm, east of the railway, has some splendid, tall trees and a round whitewashed stone and slate horse-gin building by the road. Inside this type of building, horses were yoked to the driving beam of a mill and made to walk round in circles, transmitting their power to the drive-shaft of the mill – usually for threshing grain. Opposite the farm is an old pack-horse bridge over the Evan Water, partly hidden among the trees. It has been superseded by a nearby bridge where our side road comes to a T-junction. Turn left across this bridge for the continuation of the Way.

The Old Brig Inn and the Beattock House Hotel and camping site are on opposite sides of the bridge. Beattock village is south of the bridge – to the right at the junction. Moffat is to the left – 2km (1½ miles) north-east of the bridge – and is the main tourist centre for the area, with a wide range of services.

Walkers are back on a bus route now, with food, shelter and diversions to hand. It is a good time for resting, replenishing provisions and recharging the batteries for the hard work ahead. There are many twists to the trail and much uphill work before the Way is won to the Tweed Valley and the Border towns on the route. Both east and west-bound walkers have an impressive distance behind them by the time they reach Annandale. They have much to eagerly anticipate in the distance ahead, as geographically and culturally the east and west sides of Scotland are uniquely different. From the wilds of Galloway, the scenery has been changing subtly through Kendale and Nithsdale to Annandale. For the east-bound walker, the high hills of the Borders lie ahead now, with their own special blend of magic. Whether you travel east or west from Annandale, the journey will be novel, stimulating and adventurous. If you are going the whole Way, coast-to-coast, you have reached the Great Divide, whether your sights are set on the North Sea – or on the views across the water to Ireland. The Southern Upland Way walker's education is but half complete.

Appendix I
SELECT BIBLIOGRAPHY

Fact or Fiction?
In describing the rich heritage of the Southern Uplands in this guide, an attempt has been made to distil the culture of centuries from a wide variety of sources. Legend, folklore and propaganda are all bound into a people's culture, along with documented fact. It can be extremely difficult to disentangle one from the other – even when official papers are consulted. This guide has sought to steer a careful course through this minefield, qualifying its statements with cautionary scepticism where a tale is worth telling, though its source may be elusive. To ignore the unsubstantiated legend completely is as foolish as to accept official documents uncritically. The lines of study suggested by a traverse of the Southern Upland Way are so rich and diverse that no student could possibly exhaust them in a lifetime's research. The books listed below may, however, provide a starting point for the enthusiast.

The Southern Uplands (West): Portpatrick to Beattock

Bell, David E. T. (1970). *The Highway Man.* The Ayrshire Post, Ayr.

Corrie, J. M. *The Droving Days in the South Western District of Scotland.* J. Maxwell & Son, Dumfries.

Dick, Rev. C. H. (1972). *Highways and Byways in Galloway and Carrick.* E.P. Publishing.

Edlin, Herbert L. (1974). *Forestry Commission Guide – Galloway Forest Park.* HMSO.

Harper, Malcolm McL. (1896). *Rambles in Galloway.* Thomas Fraser, Dalbeattie.

McBain, J. (1980). *The Merrick and the Neighbouring Hills.* Jackson & Sproat, Ayr.

McCormick, Andrew (1937). *Galloway: The Spell of its Hills and Glens.* John Smith & Son (Glasgow) Ltd.

MacHaffie, Fraser G. (1975). *The Short Sea Route*. T. Stephenson & Sons Ltd., Prescot.
Taylor, William (1976). *The Military Roads in Scotland*. David & Charles.
Thorne, H. D. (1976). *Rails to Portpatrick*. T. Stephenson & Sons Ltd., Prescot.
Transactions of the Dumfriesshire and Galloway Natural History Society – Wanlockhead and Leadhills Volume. Third Series, Vol. LIV (1979).

General

Andrew, K. M. and Thrippleton, A. A. (1972). *The Southern Uplands*. Scottish Mountaineering Trust.
Edlin, Herbert L. (1969). *Forests of Central and Southern Scotland*. HMSO.
Feachem, Richard (1977). *Guide to Prehistoric Scotland*. Batsford Ltd.
Geikie, Archibald (1901). *The Scenery of Scotland*. Macmillan & Co.
Glasgow Archaeological Journal, Vol. 4 – *Studies in Roman Archaeology* (1976).
Haldane, A. R. B. (1971). *The Drove Roads of Scotland*. Edinburgh University Press.
Manley, Gordon (1975). *Climate and the British Scene*. Collins.
Margery, I. D. *Roman Roads in Britain*.
Millman, R. N. (1975). *The Making of the Scottish Landscape*. Batsford Ltd.
Moir, D. G. (1975). *Scottish Hill Tracks: Old Highways and Drove Roads. (I) Southern Scotland*. Bartholomew & Son Ltd.
Murray, J. and Pullar, L. (1910). *Bathymetrical Survey of the Scottish Freshwater Lochs*, Vols 1–2.
Natural Environment Research Council (IGS) (1971). *British Regional Geology: The South of Scotland*. HMSO.
Pearsall, W. H. (1968). *Mountains and Moorlands*. Collins.
Scissons, J. B. (1967). *The Evolution of Scotland's Scenery*. Oliver & Boyd.
Stamp, L. Dudley (1969). *Britain's Structure and Scenery*. Collins.
Thomas, J. (1971). *A Regional History of the Railways of Great Britain: Vol. 6 Scotland – The Lowland and the Borders*. David & Charles.
Weir, Tom (1972). *The Scottish Lochs 2*. Constable.

Readers are also reminded of the inventories of ancient monuments, transactions of the local history societies, the county histories, and the various editions of the Statistical Accounts for the counties of Wigtown, Kirkcudbright, Dumfries, Lanark, Selkirk, Peebles, Roxburgh and Berwick, as sources of further information.

Scottish Long-Distance Footpaths

Aitken, Robert (1984). *The West Highland Way* (revised edition). HMSO.

Andrew, Ken (1984). *The Southern Upland Way*. Vol. II (East). HMSO.

Appendix II

ACKNOWLEDGEMENTS

The Southern Upland Way is the end product of a great amount of thought, discussion, documentation and hard physical work, involving many people with a wide range of talents. The Countryside Commission for Scotland has worked closely with landowners, farmers and foresters along the whole length of the Way, with the local authorities in southern and central Scotland, the Forestry Commission and other statutory bodies; with units of the army, the Scottish Conservation Projects volunteers, and numerous individuals. The author of this guide wishes to pay tribute to the many people involved in devising and creating this fine route. As a latecomer to the team, the author has not had the time or opportunity to meet all of those concerned with the project, and he may never know all their names.

I would like to thank the librarians, foresters, landowners and others who have helped me personally. It is impossible to single out individuals for credit, but, without them all, the Southern Upland Way – and this guide – would have remained ideas rather than becoming realities.

Ken Andrew
Prestwick 1983

Government Bookshops
13a Castle Street, Edinburgh EH2 3AR
49 High Holborn, London WC1V 6HB
Brazennose Street, Manchester M60 8AS
Southey House, Wine Street, Bristol BS1 2BQ
258 Broad Street, Birmingham B1 2HE
80 Chichester Street, Belfast BT1 4JY

Government publications are also available through booksellers

The waymark symbol used by the Countryside Commission for Scotland for long-distance footpaths in Scotland

Published for the Countryside Commission for Scotland by Her Majesty's Stationery Office, Edinburgh

Countryside Commission for Scotland
Battleby, Redgorton
Perth PH1 3EW

Printed in Scotland for Her Majesty's Stationery Office by Bell and Bain Ltd., Glasgow